The Character Of
An Upright Man

by

Richard Steele, M. A.
Minister of the Gospel
(Author of *A Remedy for Wandering Thoughts in the Worship
of God* and *The Religious Tradesman*)

"Jesus saw Nathanael coming to Him, and saith of him,
'Behold, an Israelite indeed, in whom is no guile.' "
John 1:47

Edited by Dr. Don Kistler

Soli Deo Gloria Publications
. . . for instruction in righteousness . . .

Soli Deo Gloria Publications
A Division of Soli Deo Gloria Ministries, Inc.
P. O. Box 451, Morgan, PA 15064
(412) 221-1901/FAX 221-1902
www.SDGbooks.com

*

The Character Of An Upright Man was first published in
1670 as *A Plain Discourse Upon Uprightness, shewing the
The Properties and Privileges of An Upright Man.* This
Soli Deo Gloria reprint, in which spelling,
grammar, and formatting changes have
been made, is © 2004 by Soli Deo Gloria.
All rights reserved. Printed in the USA.

*

ISBN 1-57358-157-7

*

Library of Congress Cataloging-in-Publication Data

Steele, Richard, 1629-1692.
  [Plain discourse upon uprightness]
  The character of an upright man / by Richard Steele ;
edited by Don Kistler.
      p. cm.
  Originally published: A plain discourse upon
uprightness. London : E. Calvert, 1670.
  ISBN 1-57358-157-7 (alk. paper)
  1. Christian life–Early works to 1800. I. Title.
BV4501.3.S737 2004
248.4'859–dc22
                                        2004005788

Contents

The Uprightness of Man

Chapter 2   47

The Uprightness of God

God shows Himself upright with an upright man:

Chapter 3   74

The Application

An Introduction to Richard Steele

Richard Steele (1629–1692) was a member of an illustrious group of practical Puritan pastors. The son of Robert Steele, a farmer, Richard was born at Barthomley, Cheshire, on May 10, 1629. He was educated at Northwich grammar school, admitted undergraduate at St. John's College, Cambridge, on April 1, 1642, and incorporated M. A. at Oxford on July 5, 1656. He succeeded Thomas Porter as rector of Hanmer, Flintshire, sometime in 1650, where Henry Newcome, a famous Puritan divine (and staunch royalist), visited him on June 10, 1654.

Steele was a member of the fourth Shropshire classis (constituted by Parliament in April 1647) and, as such, was one of the ordainers of Philip Henry on September 16, 1657. Thirty years later he was one of the ordainers of Henry's son, Matthew, the famous commentator, which took place in his own house in London. In September 1660 he was presented at the Flint assizes (a court appointed for handling offenses) for not reading *The Book of Common Prayer,* but the prosecution fell through owing to Charles's declaration of tolerance in October. The following spring Steele was again presented to the assizes, this time at Hawarden, on March 28, 1661. He resigned his living due to the Act of Uniformity in 1662 and preached a farewell sermon, never published, in which he stated that he was ejected for not subscribing to a prayer book that he had not yet seen.

Despite being deprived of his office as minister, Steele was allowed to administer the sacrament of the

Lord's Supper at Hanmer. On April 19, 1663, certain judgments were passed against him at Hanmer, but their content I have been unable to uncover. On July 25 he was questioned for baptizing his own children, and in October was arrested for suspicion of treason. Early in 1665 he was made collector for Hanmer of the "royal-aid," the point being to treat him as a layman. In April 1665 he was arrested as he was setting out for London; his pocket diary was taken from him, and passages were misconstrued. An entry discussing an appointment "on a carnal account" was interpreted to be some kind of adulterous affair. Philip Henry recorded that a great noise was heard in the country concerning the controversy. The matter was dismissed, however, as Steele had a good reputation for being a devoted husband and loving father.

On March 25, 1666, when "The Five Mile Act"* came into force, Steele was compelled to leave Hanmer; consequently he took residence in London, where he stayed his remaining years. Little is known about Steele's last years other than that he gave himself continually to the ministry of the gospel. And though he may have made occasional visits to the north, Philip Henry's diary shows that he was constantly working in London from 1671. Steele was never silenced from verbally proclaiming the riches of God's Word; he gathered a morning congregation at Armourers' Hall, Coleman Street, and in the afternoon preached at Hogsden.

On November 14, 1692, Steele visited several friends in London. He had suffered from tuberculosis for several years, according to George Hamond, but, neverthe-

---

* For a full transcription of "The Five Mile Act," go to the Soli Deo Gloria Ministries website (sdgbooks.com), and find the "Meet the Puritans" section.

less lived an active life. In the evening he retired to a
friend's house in Cheapside, where his health suddenly
deteriorated. He was carried home in a coach around
ten o'clock that night. The following day he was somewhat revived, but continued to be weak and short of
breath. His physician and close friend did all he could
for him and resigned the matter to the Lord. The next
day, on November 16, in his sixty-fourth year, Steele entered the celestial city. Hamond, his colleague and suc-
cessor, preached the funeral sermon, "A Good Minister
of Jesus Christ," in which he urged Steele's congregation not only to hear but to emulate their late pastor's
example. Steele had ten sons, five of whom had died by
1672. The historian Edmund Calamy Jr. called Steele "a
very valuable and useful man, a good scholar, a hard
student, and an excellent preacher."

Steele was preaching on the attributes of God just
weeks prior to his death. The Sabbath before he died he
presented a "rich mine of spiritual treasures" on the
goodness of God. His last words were: "You cannot
make a better choice, and are eternally undone if you
make a worse one." His assistant in the ministry wrote:
"The contemplation of the attributes of God must have
filled him with ravishment while he viewed them,
though but as in a glass, darkly; but now he is gone to
those regions of light and love where all mists are dis-
pelled; and there he has such a knowledge of them as
they who are muffled up with mortality cannot com-
prehend."

As a minister, Steele was like Caleb: he was "a man
of another spirit." He was constant in preaching, and
commonly practiced rigid study. His manuscript notes
were many, but have apparently been lost. In addition
to his sermons, he compiled and edited several treatises
(noted below). He studied to approve himself to God in
all things, and cared for his flock as a compassionate

shepherd. As can be seen from his writings, he was skilled in expounding God's Word and had rare insight into the human heart.

Most of Steele's works were sermons rewritten and expanded for the press. His most famous work, *An Antidote Against Distractions; or, An Endeavor to Serve the Church in the Daily Case of Wanderings in the Worship of God,* published in 1667 (and reissued in 1988 as *A Remedy for Wandering Thoughts in the Worship of God* by Sprinkle Publications of Harrisonburg, VA) underwent several editions. Based on 1 Corinthians 7:35, *An Antidote Against Distractions* provides the much needed corrective to intrusive, unwanted, and distracting thoughts in the worship of God. Strikingly, the work was written while Steele was in a Welsh prison, suffering for nonconformity. Between pen and sleep, he witnessed to the guards, anxious for their soul's eternal welfare.

Characteristic of his works is the stress on the vitals of religion and the heart-piety that distinguished the Puritans. Steele's *Remedy* is every bit as probing and practical as Nathaniel Vincent's *The Cure of Distractions in Attending upon God,* published in 1695, and intended for republication by Soli Deo Gloria. For those tormented by unruly thoughts, Steele's work is more than helpful. Especially astute is the author's admonition that in order to be made better, one must want to get better.

Steele published six treatises and several sermons. A collected edition was never issued from the press, but all of them were printed within the span of twenty years by various London printers. His treatises were: *An Antidote against Distractions* (1667); *The Husbandman's Calling* (1668); *A Plain Discourse upon Uprightness, Showing the Properties and Privileges of an Upright Man* (1670); *The Tradesman's Calling* (1684); and *A Discourse Concerning Old-Age* (1688). George Hamond also listed among his works the anonymous *A Scheme and Abstract of the Christian Religion* (1684). Samuel Annesley, John Wesley's maternal grandfather, published several of Steele's sermons (some as part of the casuistical *Morning Exercises*). Among them, Steele preached "The Duties of Husbands and Wives" (1674); "The Believer's Right to the Cup in the Lord's Supper" (1675); "What Are the Hindrances and Helps to a Good Memory in Spiritual Things" (1683); and "How May the Uncharitable and Dangerous Contentions that are Amongst Professors of the True Religion Be Allayed?" (1689).

The best printing of Steele's discourse on uprightness is the second London edition, printed for Edward Calvert. Soli Deo Gloria has here reproduced the 1672 edition in modern typeface. While the spelling has been somewhat modernized, the text remains largely unaltered. The result is an edition that honors the historical document, and yet is accessible to the modern reader.

A Plain Discourse upon Uprightness, containing the substance of many sermons, was written for a readership broader than Steele's own congregation. The fact that the Bishop of Chichester, Robert Grove (1634–1696), an opponent of nonconformity in nearly all its forms, gave his imprimatur ("let it be printed") to Steele's treatise shows its broad reaching spectrum.

Written for the advancement of the "vitals of genuine piety," Steele scorned undue controversies, which, he said, "scorch up all true love and zeal, and greatly grieve such as love peace." If all parties could unite to promote the honor, love, and fear of God, and the furtherance of holiness, they would soon agree or at least indulge one another in the lesser things, said Steele. He wrote, "Tis hypocrites on all sides that make our wound incurable." Thus, in many ways, *A Plain Discourse upon Uprightness* was intended to moderate the fiery debate between Conformists and Nonconformists with a true call to authentic religion. In this way Steele was much of the same spirit as Jeremiah Burroughs, earnestly desiring the unity of torn, scandalized, churches.

There are three chapters in *A Plain Discourse upon Uprightness*. The first treats the uprightness of man, the second the uprightness of God, and the third contains Steele's application of the first two. Characteristic of Puritan style, there is something for everyone in these pages. The faithful Christian will find encouragement, strength, and a road map to godliness; the backsliding believer will be able to see where to set his or her mark, and the danger of delaying repentance; and finally, the unbeliever will notice the goodness, mercy, and compassion of the Christian life, and may, by divine grace, be stirred to jealousy, to seek those things which are above.

Though the book is old, the matter it addresses and the urgency of uprightness is contemporary. Steele argued that it is impossible to be a Christian and not live (or strive to live) uprightly. The hypocrite must remain on slippery ground. Steele put it this way: "You see a spider's web to be a very curious work, but its origin is from a spider's bowels, and its design is to catch poor flies; and though she is as secure in it as in a castle, yet, when the broom comes, down they go." When God comes in judgment, the hypocrite must forever be undone.

Today too many Christians live carelessly. Backsliding from God, they lose sense of the beauty and lure of upright living. Steele admonished his readers to "read and think, and read and pray, and then through His grace it shall be useful to you."

This work is best read with pen in hand. Underline, check, and jot little notes in the margins. Ponder its words and reflect upon its meaning, but above all live it.

For its depth and evangelical fire, *A Plain Discourse upon Uprightness* should be consulted over and over for spiritual direction. We owe a great debt to Don Kistler for mining this treasure from the great Puritan caverns, and for providing us with such seasonable help in the pursuit of uprightness. It is my prayer that this book will be useful in guiding many of Zion's sons and daughters to their heavenly abode!

Randall Pederson
Grand Rapids, MI
May 2004

The Epistle to the Reader

Friendly Reader,

This small book hopes for your acceptance, merely for its honesty and plainness, which I have chiefly studied all along; a plain discourse being most fitting on plainness of heart. I am not ignorant of the various and excellent tracts on this subject, unto which little substance can be added, especially by me, who has so little mental or experimental insight into the point in hand. If a friendly violence had not been used upon me, this would never have appeared. But my flexible disposition could not, without flat incivility, withstand the undeniable importunities of a very grave, judicious minister who (upon hearing some headings hereof delivered) would not rest without my promise to make it public. I thought it unworthy of the press but, being thus engaged I could not go back, and thereupon enlarging the matter and slightly altering the method, I have at last sent it out. May the blessing of God be with it. A man may preach profitably on those points that have heretofore been handled; and it is possible to print acceptably on subjects written on before, especially where some variety of matter and variation of method is added, which I hope you will find in this piece in hand.

Moreover there are such swarms of litigious books of controversies, which scorch up all true love and zeal, and greatly grieve such as love peace, that may perhaps make such discourses as this concerning the vital parts of genuine piety to be very necessary. For certainly, if our ends were right, and our hearts upright with our God; if Christian magistrates, ministers, and people were plainly and truly bent to promote the honor, love, and fear of God, and the indubitable ways of holiness, we would soon agree, or else charitably indulge one another in these lesser things. It is the hypocrites on all sides that make our wounds incurable. Surely where the mind is sound and the heart sincere in the main, grains of allowance should be granted for some errors of the understanding and failings in the conduct—lest we deal with others as we would be loath to be dealt with either by God or men. The consideration hereof, and also of the scarcity of sincere Christians compared to the plenty of hypocrites in the world, may make some tolerable apology for this small tract, which I most earnestly recommend, first to the blessing of the Lord and then to your diligent perusal. Read and think, and read and pray, and then through His grace it shall be useful to you.

And I beseech you, for the Lord Jesus' sake and for the love of the Spirit, strive together with me in your prayers to God for me, a miserable sinner, that I may be upright and useful till I die, whereby you will abundantly recompense these endeavors of your servant in the gospel,

Richard Steele
October 1, 1670

Chapter 1

The Upright Man

"With the upright, Thou wilt show Thyself upright."
Psalm 18:25

Section 1: The context

He who would be wise, let him read Proverbs. He who would be holy, let him read the Psalms. Every line in this book breathes peculiar sanctity.

This psalm, though placed among the first ones, was penned among the last (as the preface assures us) and is left as the epitome of the general history of David's life. It is twice recorded in the Scripture (2 Samuel 22:26 and in this Book of Psalms) for its excellency and sweetness. Surely we should take double notice of it then.

Holy David, being near the shore, here looks on his former dangers and deliverances with a thankful heart, and writes this psalm to bless the Lord. It is as if each of you who have grown into years should review your lives and observe the wonderful goodness and providence of God towards you; and then sit down and write a modest memorial of his most remarkable mercies to comfort yourselves and your posterity, which would be an excellent practice. What a comfort it would be for you to read how good your God was to your father or grandfather, who are now dead and gone! So would your children rejoice in the Lord upon reading of His goodness to you. And you cannot have a better pattern for this than holy David, who wrote this psalm when he was sixty-seven years old. When he had outlived most of his troubles

1

and was almost ready for his journey to his Father in heaven, he resolved to leave this good report of Him on earth.

Mark how he begins: he does not set up trophies to himself, but triumphs in his God. "I will love Thee, O Lord, my strength." As the love of God is the beginning of all our mercies, so love for God should be the end and effect of them all. As the stream leads us to the spring, so all the gifts of God must lead us to the giver of them. "Lord, Thou hast saved me from sickness, so I will love Thee; from death and hell, so I will love Thee. On me Thou hast bestowed grace and comfort, so I will love Thee, O Lord my strength." And later he heaped on God all the sweet names he could devise (verse 2). A true saint thinks he can never speak too well of God or too ill of himself. And then he begins his narrative.

• Of his dangers (verses 4–5): snares of death, floods of ungodly men, and sorrows of hell. Hell and earth are combined against each holy man, and will trouble him sufficiently in this world if they cannot keep him out of a better one.

• Of his retreat, and that was earnest prayer to God. Verse 6: "I called upon the Lord, and cried unto my God." When our prayers are ardent and importunate, then they speed. "My cry came before Him, even into His ears." The mother trifles while the child whimpers; but when he raises his note, strains every nerve, and tries every vein, then she throws all aside and gives him his desire. While our prayers are only whispers, our God can take His rest; but when we fall to crying, "Now will I arise," says the Lord.

• Of his rescue (verses 7–20): by the powerful and terrible arm of the Lord, who is in a lofty strain, brought in to His servant's help, as if He would mingle heaven and earth together rather than leave His child in the lion's paws.

• Of the reason for this gracious dealing of God with him (verse 20 and following): he was a righteous person, and he had a righteous cause. And thereupon he turned to God, saying, "Thou hast dealt with me just as Thou art wont to do; for with the merciful Thou wilt shew Thyself merciful; and with the upright man Thou wilt shew Thyself upright."

Section 2: The text opened
So we arrive at the text itself, which is an entire proposition containing a subject (an upright man), a predicate, or what is spoken of him, to, or with him (God will show Himself upright), and an explication (with, before, or unto him).

"Upright." The same word is often translated "perfect." An upright man is good throughout, though not thoroughly good; he is not one who personifies religion, but one who is a religious person. He is perfect because he wishes to be so. So Noah is termed in Genesis 6:9: "Noah was a just man, and perfect (i.e., upright) in his generations, and Noah walked with God." He was a good man in a bad age. He was like a glowing spark of fire in a sea of water, which is perfect goodness; and therefore the Holy Ghost so hangs upon his name as if he could not stop saying it. Verse 10: "And Noah begat three sons." It is as if God were saying, "Noah, Noah, Noah, I love the sound of your name." And so all our names are precious to God, though hated by men, if the name of God is dear and sweet to us.

The word is also sometimes translated "plain." In Genesis 25:27, Jacob was a plain man, that is, an upright man, dwelling in tents. Esau was a cunning hunter, but Jacob was a plain man. You might know his heart by his tongue, save once when Rebeccah put a cunning trick into his head; otherwise he was a most upright, downright man. And the plain meaning of it is a simple, cordial, unfeigned and exact man—this is the man we are looking for.

"Man." This substantive the Hebrews usually drown in the adjective, but here the Holy Ghost exhibits a word, and a choice one too, signifying a strong, valiant man. The same word is used in Psalm 45:3: "O mighty [man]!" It is meant of our Lord Christ, who was a most strong and valiant man, who could meet the wrath of God, the malice of the devil, and the sin of man in the face, and come off with triumph. The Dutch translate the clause in 2 Samuel 22:26 this way: "With the right, valiant person, Thou behavest Thyself upright."

In short, if the words were literally translated, they would run thus: "a man of uprightnesses," that is, every way you behold him, he is an upright man; like an even dye, cast him whichever way you will, he will be found square and right; a stiff and strong man to tread down both lusts within and temptations without. He is like Athanasius against the world or Luther against Rome. He is a man of an excellent spirit, and such is our upright man.

"Thou wilt show Thyself upright," or, "Thou wilt be upright with him," for one word in the Hebrew makes all these six English words: "Thou wilt upright it with him." If men will deal plainly with God, He will deal plainly with them. He who is upright in performing his duty shall find God upright in performing His promises. It is God's way to carry with men as they carry with Him. If you have a design to please Him, He will have a design to please you; if you will echo to Him when He calls, He will echo to you when you call. On the other hand, if a man will wrestle with God, He will wrestle with him; if you will be fast and loose with Him, and walk frowardly towards Him, you shall have it as good as you bring it. If you provoke Him with never-

ending sins, He will pursue you with never-ending torments. If you will sin for eternity, you must suffer for
eternity. Every man shall find like for like.

Section 3: The doctrine stated

And now it is time to be gathering something for
our instruction, and let this be the lesson hence to be
learned.

**DOCTRINE: Where God finds an upright man, He
shows Himself to be an upright God.**

True, He finds none but whom He makes. He finds
them of His own making; but wherever such a man is
found, on the throne, in a prison, or on a dunghill, he
shall find a God of his own who will deal uprightly with
him. He is an upright God; let men be what they will;
whatever contrary motions the lower spheres have, yet
the *primum mobile* keeps its even and constant motion
and is never diverted out of its course at all. So is it with
our God: let vain hypocrites walk never so crookedly, yet
the holy God will be justified when He speaks and clear
when He judges. He will be upright with you in execut-
ing His threatenings if you hinder the current of His
uprightness in performing promises. The filthy dunghill cannot infect the glorious sun that shines all day
upon it, nor can any man's evil cause him to cease from
being good. But the meaning of the point is, to the upright man He shows Himself to be a graciously upright
God. A true-hearted man on earth shall find a true-
hearted God in heaven.

The most proper and profitable way I can think of to
handle this doctrine within the intended limits is, first,
by showing wherein the uprightness of a man stands;
second, by declaring how God shows Himself to be an
upright God; and, third, by drawing out some infer-
ences and uses thereof.

Section 4: Words for "uprightness" in Scripture

There are four words especially whereby uprightness is expressed in Scripture which, being considered, will give us some view of this orient jewel.

1. It is called "truth." 1 Samuel 12:24: "Serve Him in truth." Moral truth is the conformity of the mind and heart to things said and done; when therefore the heart prays with the tongue, when the heart obeys with the hand, when we do the things of God heartily as to the Lord, this is to serve Him in truth and uprightly.

This surely is the sense of Hebrews 10:22: "Let us draw near with a true heart." It is our sin and folly to keep at distance from God, both in and out of His service, afraid or loath to come near. It is God's will that we should draw near, and nearer yet, and that with a true heart. A true-hearted man at prayer does the work when many great appearances are but beating the air.

So it is when we come to men. 1 John 3:18: "Let us not love in word neither in tongue [only], but in deed and in truth," having a principle of unfeigned love in our hearts to everybody, and thence producing words and deeds of pure charity. This is an upright man, whose heart within does not give the lie to his word and actions. Survey his duties to God and men, they are pious, just, and charitable; open his heart, and piety, righteousness, and love are written there. One man professed that if he might have had the opportunity to make himself, light would have been his body and truth would have been his soul.

2. Another word for this is "sincerity," a word taken from pure honey. The Latin is *sine cera*, without wax or unmingled. The equivalent for us would be when the new man has as little as may be of the old man mingled with him. This word is used in Philippians 1:10: "That ye may be sincere." The Greek word there signifies that which is sunproof (such as wares that can abide be

tried between you and the sun). Such is an upright man: bring him to the Scriptures and he is sound; bring him to any solid marks and he can stand before them; put him on the scales and he is the right weight. He is pure gold, though he may lack some grains of allowance. He is of a right breed; though perhaps young or weak; yet he can look at the Sun and not be daunted. A hypocrite can look men in the face, but an upright man can look God in the face. "As for me, I will behold Thy face in righteousness." This none but a righteous upright man can do.

3. There is another word of this import, and that is "singleness of heart." Acts 2:46: "They did eat their meat with gladness and singleness of heart," that is, with a cordial cheerfulness and bounty. To this Luke 11:34 refers: "When thine eye is single [when your heart is singly bent to honor and serve God, then the whole life will relish of that principle], thy whole body also is full of light." But if the heart doubles with God, the life will in no way be uniform with men. And this is taken to be the meaning of the oneness of heart promised in Ezekiel 11:19. The hypocrite has a heart, a heart, a heart, and a heart, for every lust a heart; a double-minded man is unstable in all his ways. He is unresolved in the end he drives at, and so unfixed in his desires and actions that tend thereunto. Now the upright man's heart is one; he goes all one way; he is what he seems; he has one intention, one delight, one face, and one tongue. In a word, he is one united man. Psalm 103:1: "Bless the Lord, O my soul, and *all* that is within me bless His holy Name."

And to this purpose is the fourth word that signifies uprightness, and that is "integrity." 1 Kings 9:4: "And if thou wilt walk before Me, as David, thy father, walked, in integrity of heart, and in uprightness." That is when all the soul in every faculty is resolved and bent for God and His glory. In a hypocrite, the judgment is against the will, the conscience against the affection, and the reason against the appetite. But in the upright, all the faculties agree and combine within themselves, and the opposition is only outward, against a common enemy. He is a whole man and is for the whole will of God.

So you see that an upright man is a true-hearted, a sincere-hearted, a single-hearted, and a whole-hearted man.

Section 5: The ground of uprightness

This uprightness respects God and respects man. The former may be called "uprightness of heart," the latter "uprightness of life." And both of these must be explained; and, where they meet, there we find an upright man.

Concerning uprightness of heart, we must assert that it is not so much a distinct grace, a grace by itself, as it is all grace. It is that which stamps a reality on every other grace. Without it, we cannot believe our faith, nor love our love, nor hope well of our hope itself.

Uprightness and watchfulness are universal graces; they are of a general necessity. Uprightness is necessary to the being and truth of grace, and watchfulness is necessary to the preservation and exercise of grace. And on that account, sincerity is called a girdle in Ephesians 6:14: "Having your loins girded about with truth." Religion is to many as a cloak (though it will prove the dearest cloak that ever was worn) which they can put on when it serves their purposes, and put off when it troubles them in their lust. But sincerity is like a girdle that ties it close to us. This makes all our garments fit close to us, and to be ungirt here is to be unblessed.

Uprightness of heart is that grace or gracious temper whereby the soul is unreservedly resigned to God, and heartily bent to walk with Him without guile. In short, it is when one is a man after God's own heart; for truth is nothing but an agreement of things with their first principles, so that the heart that agrees plainly with the heart and will of God is an upright heart.

The same thing is meant by an honest heart in Luke 8:15. That is a heart resolved to carry squarely towards God. Such a heart, in the hearing of God's Word, is clearly carried with the stream of God's will, without exception or dissimulation. As an honest man is ruled and swayed by reason and equity in a business, without squinting at his own opinions and ends, even so an upright heart honestly yields his reason and will captive to the will of God, though it cross his own conceits and ends. And thus he is a man after God's own heart, is as like Him (human frailty considered) as ever he can be.

This blessed uprightness may be considered in its grounds, in its nature, and in its object.

The ground and root of uprightness of heart stands in the total receiving of Christ by the heart, and the total resignation of the heart to Him. When this is done, a good foundation is laid for sincerity of soul.

First, there must be a total receiving of Jesus Christ as offered in the gospel; this is when you take hold of the Lord Jesus and cleave to Him with purpose of heart. Barnabas pressed them at Antioch to this in Acts 11:23. Many have a month's mind of Christ, some wishes and woulds, but will you have Him and cleave to Him, and that with purpose of heart? Sincerity is to receive a whole Christ with a whole heart. It is not to receive Christ the Savior or Refuge only, or most would be willing, but Christ the Prince and Portion also in the land of the living. So David could say in Psalm 142:5, "O Lord, Thou art my Refuge, and my Portion in the land of the living." But how many would have the Lord Jesus Christ for their Refuge when conscience pinches,

affliction presses, or death stares them in the face; and
how few will choose Him for their Portion and happiness in the midst of their outward comforts? The hypocrite dares not die without Him, and the upright saint
cannot live without Him. Song of Solomon 1:4: "The
upright love Thee," and love cannot live contentedly
without fruition.

To be content with Christ because of some present
need of Him is one thing, but it is nothing if that is all.
But to choose Him as the fairest of ten thousand, and
that with an entire heart; to have mind, will, conscience, and affection all of one mind, and this mind
to be set on Christ's yoke as well as His crown, His
Spirit as well as His merit, His rule as well as His righteousness—there is the upright heart. A hypocrite has
some fancy for Jesus Christ, but will not have all of
Him. This part pleases him, but that part does not; and
so he dodges endlessly and parleys with him through
the window, but bolts the door and keeps Him out forever. Oh, that ever a holy, just, and offended God
should follow such miserable sinners with a bleeding
Christ in His arms, and that ever such wretches should
refuse Him!

There must be a total resignation of the heart unto
the Lord Jesus Christ, wherein you cordially, deliber-
ately, and freely give up your souls and bodies to Him
and His service, which is called "engaging the heart to
approach to the Lord." Jeremiah 30:21: " 'Who is this
that engaged his heart to approach unto Me?' saith the
Lord." And thereupon that happy covenant is drawn in
the next verse: "Ye shall be My people, and I will be your
God."

"Who is this?" God asks. "Who in the world? Who in
this congregation? Who in this family? Who in this
seat? Where is the man, the woman, the child?"

Oh, let each answer quickly, "It is I." But you must

engage, not only hanker, incline, desire, purpose, but engage. It is not bidding, but buying, that will make this Pearl your own. Alas, it is the ordinary guise of people to stand off and look only. But, sirs, will you engage? Is it a bargain; and will you stick to it, get or lose by it? Will you have Christ? Then there must the engagement of the heart. You subscribed your hands in baptism; this very covenant was sealed in your name and on your behalf when you were little children, and your not revoking it asserts it. But now we come for your hearts' engagement thereunto. Where is the mind, the conscience, the will? Oh, where is the will that submits, resolves, and engages to be the Lord's? Happy this day, and happy you will be, if hereupon you shall say, "I am the Lord's"; and another shall call himself by the name of Jacob, and another shall subscribe with his hand unto the Lord, and surname himself by the name of Israel (Isaiah 44:5). You are the Lord's by your Christian names already. Oh, when will you be His by your surname also?

This is the gospel's great design; this is our errand here; we come for you and are loath to go without you. We beseech you by the mercies of God to present yourselves as a living sacrifice to God. Poor sinners are like besieged rebels whom Christ Jesus will either win or starve. His ordinance is mounted and it batters. A breach is made in the judgment, but the sinner will not yield; another in the conscience, yet is he loath to yield. The white flag of mercy is set up, but for a long time the sturdy sinner will not look at it. The red flag is hung out, divine wrath is on the march, and a storm is preparing. The ordinance of God is planted again; and now if it hits right, and a breach is made upon the will, then Christ is victorious, the city is won, and the sinner yields. And then his note is changed. Psalm 116:16: "O Lord, truly I am Thy servant, I am Thy servant." Mark how the psalmist doubles it, as if to say, "I am, I am, truly I am." Doubled refusals call for doubled submissions.

The sinner must say, "I will neither be my own master nor my own servant. I here make a deed of gift of my whole self to Thee without reservation, and without power of revocation." It is not enough to say this in a pang of kindness, or in a compliment, as we do to men. What is more common with us than to say, "I am your servant, sir"? But it is a servant without service, and God has a great many such servants. They are His servants, but their own masters. But holy David was not such a man. "I am Thy servant, truly I am Thy servant. I am resigned to Thee, I am resolved for Thee. Thou hast boared [opened] my ears (Psalm 40:6) and obliged me to Thee forever. I will be Thine totally and finally."

When you give yourselves to the Lord in this way (2 Corinthians 8:5), this is the ground and root of uprightness.

Section 6: The nature of uprightness
The nature of this uprightness of heart is best discerned by those expressions used by the Holy Ghost concerning it, which have been partly observed already, and shall be reduced to these following. Uprightness of heart is:
1. Single without division
2. Sound without rottenness
3. Pure without mixture
4. Perfect without reservation
5. Plain without guile.

1. An upright heart is single without division. To a hypocrite, there are many gods and many lords, and he must have a heart for each. But to the upright there is but one God the Father and one Lord Jesus Christ, and one heart will serve them both. He who fixes his heart

upon the creature, for every creature he must have a heart, and the dividing of his heart destroys him (Hosea 10:2). Worldly profits knock at the door, and he must have a heart for them; carnal pleasures present themselves, and he must have a heart for them also; sinful preferments appear, and they must have a heart too. Of necessary objects, the number is few; of needless vanities, the number is endless. The upright man has made choice of God and has enough.

A single Christ is enough for a single heart; hence holy David prayed in Psalm 86:11: "Unite my heart to fear Thy name." That is, "Let me have but one heart and mind, and let that be Thine."

As there are thousands of beams and rays, yet they all meet and center in the sun. So an upright man, though he has a thousand thoughts, yet they all (by his good will) meet in God. He has many subordinate ends—to procure a livelihood, to preserve his credit, to provide for his children—but he has no supreme end but God alone. Hence he has that steadiness in his res- olutions, that undistractedness in his holy duties, that consistency in his actions, and that evenness in the frame of his heart, which miserable hypocrites cannot attain.

2. An upright heart is sound without rottenness. Psalm 119:80: "Let my heart be sound in Thy statutes, that I may not be ashamed." The more sincerity, the less shame. Integrity is the great author of confidence. Every frost shakes an unsound body, and every trial shakes an unsound soul. An upright man does not al- ways have so pure a color as a hypocrite may have, but his color is natural; it is his own; it is not painted; his constitution is firm. The hypocrite's beauty is bor- rowed; the fire of trial will melt it off.

An upright man has his infirmities, his diseases, but his new nature works them out for he is sound within.

A leprosy overspreads the hypocrite, but he hides it. Psalm 36:2: "He flattereth himself in his own eyes, until his iniquity be found to be hateful." He endeavors to hide himself from God, more from men, but most from himself. He would fain be in with himself howsoever, and this trade he drives "till his iniquity be found to be hateful." But an upright man is always sifting and trying himself: "Am I sound? Am I right? Are my services rightly done? Are my infirmities consistent with integrity?" An upright saint is like an apple with rotten specks, but a hypocrite is like the apple with a rotten core.

The sincere Christian has a speck of passion here, there one of worldliness, and there one of pride. But cut him up and anatomize him, and he is sound at heart; there Christ and Christianity live and reign. A hypocrite is like an apple that is smooth and lovely on the outside, but rotten within. His words may be exact, his duties devout, and his life blameless; but look within, and his heart is the sty of sin, the den of Satan.

3. An upright heart is pure without mixture. It is not absolutely pure, for that happy condition is reserved for heaven; but it is compared with the pollution and base mixture that constitutes a hypocrite. Though his hand cannot do all that God bids, yet his heart is sincere in all he does. His soul is bent for perfect purity, and so he has his name from that. Matthew 5:8: "Blessed are the pure in heart." In his words he sometimes fails, and also in his thoughts and deeds; but open his heart and there is a love, a desire, a design and an endeavor after real and absolute purity. He is not legally pure, that is, free from all sin, but he is evangelically pure, free from the reign of all sin, especially of hypocrisy, which is so flatly contrary to the covenant of grace. And in this sense the upright man is the Scripture Puritan, and so is further from hypocrisy than any other man. He is

really glad that God is the Searcher of hearts, for then he knows that he will find His name and nature in his own.

And yet the most upright man in the world has some hypocrisy in him. Proverbs 20:9: "Who can say, 'I have made my heart clean. I am pure from my sin'?" But he detects, resists, and hates this hypocrisy; and so it cannot denominate him as a hypocrite in this world, nor damn him as one in another. His ends are generally purely for the glory of God; his frame of heart and thoughts are pure, and generally better than his outside; the farther you trace him, the better he is. He is pure from dishonesty in his dealings, purer yet in his family from all appearance of evil, purer still in his closet, and most pure in his heart. Though there is sin there, yet there is also there an antipathy against it, so that it does not mingle with it.

The hypocrite chooses sin; the upright man would have no sin if he could choose. The traveler meets with dirt on his way, but he keeps it off as well as he can and does not mingle with it. And if he gets soiled, he rubs it off as soon as may be. But the swine delights in it and cannot be well without it. It is just so between the upright man and the hypocrite. The most upright saint on earth is mired with sin sometimes, but he did not design it in the morning, nor does he sleep with it at night. But a hypocrite designs it and delights in it; he is never so well contented as in sin. In a word, the hypocrite may avoid sin, but no man can abhor sin save the upright man.

4. An upright man is perfect and entire without reservation. Psalm 37:37: "Mark the perfect man, and behold the upright." You may see them both at once. His heart is entirely devoted to the will and ways of God. The hypocrite ever has some exceptions and reservations. "Such a sin I must not leave; such a grace I can-

not love; such a duty I will not practice. Thus far I will yield but no farther; thus far I will go. It is consistent with my carnal ends, but all the world shall not persuade me farther." The judgment of the hypocrite will drive beyond his will, his conscience beyond his affections; he is not entire, his heart is parted, and so he is off and on.

The upright man has but one happiness, and that is the enjoyment of God; he has but one rule, and that is His holy will; he has but one work, and that is to please his Maker. Thereupon he is entire and certain in his choices, in his desires, in his ways and contrivances. And though there may be some demurs in his prosecution of his main business, yet there is no hesitancy and wavering between two objects; for he is entirely fixed and resolved therein, and so may be said to be "perfect and entire, wanting nothing."

There is in every hypocrite some one fort or stronghold that has never yielded to the sovereignty and empire of God's will. Some lust fortifies itself in the will; but where integrity enters, it brings every thought into captivity to the obedience of Christ. "Lord," he says, "I am wholly Thine; do what Thou wilt with me; say what Thou wilt to me; write what Thou wilt upon me. 'Other lords besides Thee have had dominion over us, but by Thee only we will make mention of Thy name' " (Isaiah 26:13). Here is the upright man.

5. An upright heart is plain without guile. Psalm 32:2: "Blessed is the man to whom the Lord imputeth not iniquity, and in whose spirit there is no guile." Here is a blessed word indeed. Alas! We have great and many iniquities; would it not be happy for us to be as if we had never sinned? Why, non-imputation will be as well for us as if there had been no transgression; sins remitted are as if they had not been committed; the debt-book crossed as good as if no entries had ever

been made. But who is this blessed man? "In whose spirit there is no guile," that is, no fundamental guile. He is the man who has not deceitfully covenanted with his God. He has no approved guile, to approve and yield to any way of wickedness; he does not juggle with God or men or with his own conscience; he does not hide his idols under him when God is searching his tent. Rather, as it follows in verse 5, he acknowledges, hates, and leaves his sin.

When the upright man confesses his sin, his heart aches and he is deeply troubled for it; he does not dissemble. The hypocrite proclaims open war, but maintains secret intelligence with his lusts. When the upright man prays for any grace, he earnestly desires it, and he takes pains to compass it too; for he is in good earnest and does not dissemble. The hypocrite is afraid in his prayers to be taken at his word, for he does not love the image or grace of God at all. And so in everything else, there is nothing but guile in him.

He who will dissemble with God will dissemble with any man in the world. See the wide difference between Saul and David. Saul is charged with a fault in 1 Samuel 15:14. He denies it, and the charge is renewed in verse 17. Still he minces the matter and looks for fig-leaves to cover all. But plain-hearted David is another man; he is charged and he yields; one prick opens a vein of sorrow in his heart. He tells all, he makes a psalm of it, and therein concludes this in Psalm 51:6: "Behold, Thou desirest truth in the inward parts." The plain-hearted man says, "As for me, with the upright man I will show myself upright."

Section 7: The great business of the upright heart
The great business of the upright heart is inward religion, universal religion, and constant religion.

He is a student and practitioner of inward religion.

He is diligent in the outward acts of it also (that he has in common with the hypocrite), but his greatest study is to be good within. Romans 2:28–29: "For he is not a Jew who is one outwardly [that is, he is no Jew as to the esteem and acceptation of God, or as to the spiritual privileges of the covenant], neither is that circumcision which is outward in the flesh [to wit, that is not the circumcision, which God chiefly looks at, and which a man is chiefly advantaged by]; but he is a Jew who is one inwardly [that is, a saint in soul], and circumcision is that of the heart, in the spirit and not in the letter." It is not water on the face, but blood on the heart which makes a saveable Christian. O sirs, what change has there been on your spirits? What fear, love, and sanctity is there in your hearts? Look to this, or else you will break like bubbles. And then it follows, "whose praise is not of men, but of God," that is, whose aim and whose honor is not to be praised by men, but by God. The upright man trades in invisible things.

The upright man studies to obtain invisible graces. Psalm 45:13: "The king's daughter is glorious within." In the hidden man of the heart lies the beauty of an upright man: to be dressed with the ornament of a meek and quiet spirit, with a composed and serious spirit, with a penitent and believing spirit. Ah, beloved, how like many of us are to the river which Athenaeus mentions, whose upper waters are sweet, but brackish at the bottom; like fine clothes, silk without and canvas within; a smooth carriage and an unpolished, uncircumcised heart.

But the upright man would not be so. He does not look at things that are seen, but at things that are not seen. Grace and glory are the study and ambition of the inward Christian. The hypocrite may be forward for unsanctified gifts. Simon Magus would give money for such. Oh, the time, cost and strength that many men

So true!

spend to attain the gifts of knowledge, prudence, language, elocution, memory, and such like, who never spend a serious thought, to attain the graces of repentance, faith, self-denial, sincere love to God, and godliness! But this is the great design in the upright heart: "Oh, that I may be stored with the saving knowledge of my God, and of myself! Here's an ordinance. Oh, that I may have my faith increased, my love enflamed, and the back of my patience strengthened by this holy duty!" These are the pearls our merchant seeks!

2. The upright man studies to perform invisible duties. There is an outside and an inside part to religion. The bended knee is the outside part in prayer; the broken heart is the inside. To hear God's Word is the outside part; to meditate on it is the inside. To read two or three chapters in the Bible each day is the outside part; to feel the efficacy of it is the inside. To reprove another man is the outside part; but to watch over your own heart is the inside. To draw out your purse to a poor man is the outside part; but to draw out your heart in pity to him is the inside part of the duty. The hypocrite may, and often does, excel in the former, but the upright man is diligent and careful in the latter. He can pray in secret, and is no stranger to self-examination, meditation, ejaculatory prayers, and soliloquies, those retired acts of religion; nay, in these is his excellency. He is a saint in secret, the holiest when alone, a busy man in an ordinance. He wrestles as well as makes supplication, and sweats at that which others sleep at. The Pharisee in Luke 18 had the larger oration, but the publican had the more penitent heart. The scribe might have more dealing with the Law, but the apostle delighted in it in the inward man (Romans 7:22), and so does every upright man. His best wares are within, out of sight. It is the tradesman's custom to have all his wares for sale, but in his warehouse and closet are his

OUTSIDE vs. INSIDE

choicest things. Even so the upright man will be exact and diligent in all his ordinary and visible duties, but his masterpieces are within. He performs invisible duties.

3. The upright man studies to conquer invisible sins. These are the sins that he might go to his grave with, and nobody was ever aware of them; yet these he labors to rout. A hypocrite, on the contrary, prunes off the sins that will shame him, but nourishes the sins that will damn him. Open drunkenness, uncleanness, oppression, and profaneness a hypocrite disdains; but meanwhile he lives perhaps in some of these secretly, or at least takes no pains to subdue proud, wanton, envious, and other inward motions that do as much war against the soul as other sins. The hypocrite shaves the hair, but the upright man plucks it up by the roots. 2 Corinthians 7:1: "Let us cleanse ourselves from all filthiness of the flesh and spirit." There is a filthiness of the spirit which he who would perfect holiness will be cleansing himself from, such as the habits of unbelief, impenitence, hardness of heart, pride of spirit, dullness in God's service, and such sins as atheistic, loose, impertinent thoughts, wandering thoughts in the worship of God, envy at his neighbor's riches or reputation, and carnal contrivances to satisfy the lusts of the flesh. These break his sleep and fill his prayers, which never cost the hypocrite one penitent thought. The upright man knows that as the filthiness of the flesh will make him a beast, so the filthiness of the spirit will make him a devil; and therefore he assaults his invisible sins.

Section 8: An upright man labors after universal religion

The will of God is in an upright man's heart, and he agrees with Scripture in everything.

1. He hates all sin with a hatred of abomination, of

aversion, and of opposition. Dress it with what disguises you will, and press it with what motives, ends or advantages you can, the upright man hates it in his heart. Psalm 119:1, 3: "Blessed are the undefiled in the way, who walk in the Law of the Lord. They also [for their part] do no iniquity; they walk in His way." There is a part of him that would tamper with sin, but he does not likes it. " 'Oh,' saith God, 'do not this abominable thing that I hate' " (Jeremiah 44:4). "No, Lord," he says, "for I hate it as well as Thou dost." His heart is on God's side against sin, and particularly against his own iniquity. Psalm 18:23: "I was also upright before Him, and I kept myself from mine iniquity." Every man has some sin of his own to which he is most inclined, least able to resist, and most loath to leave. Thus he drags each prayer before God and cries, "Lord, if Thou lovest me, strike here!" This sin he prosecutes with prayers and tears, and all good means beside, ambushes it in cold blood, and with continual, preventing contrivances disappoints, crosses, intercepts, and by degrees starves it to death.

And as no sin is so dear as to ingratiate with him, so no sin is so small but his stomach rises at it; and hence it is that the upright man does not have so wide a inclination as other men of large and strained consciences, and so meets with many a hypocrite in his dish, because he hates the appearance of evil as he hates the appearance of the devil. But still he hates his own sins more than others, and those as much as any which nobody sees but himself.

2. He loves all his duty; he is neither afraid to know nor ashamed to own all his duty. By this the Lord measures integrity. 1 Kings 9:4: "And if thou wilt walk before Me, as David thy father walked, in integrity of heart and in uprightness, to do according to all that I have commanded thee." Here's the just standard of sincerity.

For can the holy, wise, and just God appoint anything unreasonable or uncomfortable for His own creature, His dear child to perform? Alas! All His ways are mercy and truth, and all His laws tend to His servants' good. What harsher law in appearance can there be than that found in Matthew 5:29–30: "If thy right eye, if thy right hand offend thee, pluck it out, cut it off." And yet if any of you had an eye that was always leading you into pits and precipices, to drown and destroy you, would not you have it out? If you had a hand that was always running into the fire, and you could not keep it out, would not you hack it off? Why, it is no other eye or hand the gospel has a quarrel with but those that would lead you into ruin or run you into hell—and how reasonable and necessary is it to be rid of such?

The upright man is convinced of this, and so he knows nothing in religion but what he likes. Some things may grate upon his carnal appetite, yet he loves them dearly. Now a hypocrite is quite another man; like a poor scholar reading a hard chapter, he skips over the hard words and makes nothing of them; whereas the well-taught scholar will tarry and labor at them and rather venture a whipping than skip over them. So is it between the hypocrite and the upright man in the duties of Christianity. A hypocrite runs smoothly on in divers religious exercises till he meets with some costly, hard, or hidden duties, and there he stands stock-still; he considers that there is no credit or profit, but only pains or peril to be had, and so skips over these hard words and neither loves nor obeys. But the upright man finds his duty, abides by it, dwells upon it, and will deny himself before he will deny his duty. "If God will have me love my enemies, I will love them. If He will have me forsake this company or course that I am taken with, I will freely leave them. If He will have me pray, yea, and fast too, no duty shall be so hard but I will do it, no sin so sweet but I will leave it with my whole heart and my whole soul."

We see both of these in Psalm 119:128: "Therefore I esteem all Thy precepts concerning all things to be right, and I hate every false way." Each word is a sacred touchstone.

"Therefore." It is said in verse 126 that [wicked men] "make void the law." That's so far from carrying the upright man down the stream that therefore he loves it the more; he knows it cannot but be excellent that such men hate. Is the Sabbath generally broken? He is stricter in observing it then. Are oaths more frequent? He abhors them all the more. Is true piety hated and hissed out of the world? Then his heart and house shall more thoroughly embrace it.

"I esteem." I cannot observe Thy precepts as I would, but I do dearly value them. The least of Thy Laws is more unto me than thousands of gold and silver pieces.

"I esteem Thy precepts." I not only esteem the truths of the Bible, the histories in the Bible, and the promises of the Bible, but I esteem Thy precepts, those that cut out my work as well as those that hold out my reward.

"And *all* these." This includes those that are against my nature and interest and custom as well as those that are agreeable to my nature and custom, and subservient to my interest. They are all wise, holy and good. "Thy Word is very pure; therefore Thy servant loves it. And I esteem all Thy precepts [concerning all things to be right]." Those precepts that give rules for my bargains as well as for my hearing, that control me at my table as well as those that direct me in my prayers—they are all right and good.

"And I hate every false way." I do not say that I escape and miss them all (happy I would be if I could); but I hate them, and he who hates sin, will avoid it as much as he can. And I hate *every* false way. I see they are false ways, neither directed by my God nor leading to Him, and therefore I hate them all. This is an upright man: he is universally religious.

Section 9: An upright man labors after constant religion

His sanctity is a second nature in him, and that which is natural is constant. There is a great difference between the natural heat of a healthy man and the praeternatural heat of a fever; such is the difference between the true saint and the hypocrite. A hypocrite may have some fits of piety, but they are accidental; they flow from some outward cause, and accordingly they last but for a while. And when that cause ceases (suppose some sharp judgement feared or felt, some qualm of conscience or shallow sermon-sickness), then a cold fit follows as bad or worse than before. Alas, it is praeternatural; it was no habit. But the upright man has a constant heat; he fears always and maintains constant duty, though he cannot keep equal heat therein.

And here's the difference between the inconstancy of an upright man and of a hypocrite: the inconstancy of the hypocrite is in the substance of the duty itself; one while he prays, another while he restrains prayer; one while he is strict and cautious, and another shortly loose and careless. Whereas the upright man keeps on in the course of his duty, though he cannot do it always alike. He prays, and would not be taken from it, though the thread of his prayers is uneven. There may be remissness in it, but not an intermission of it; there's constant religion, though not equal religion. The hypocrite makes a cloak of his religion, which he puts on and off as it serves his purpose; the upright man wears it as his everyday clothes, and does not put off his integrity till he dies. There may be some parentheses in his holy course wherein vanity and sin may be written (too many of these, God knows, in the best man's heart and life), but still the sentence runs current; the sense and scope of his heart runs heavenward. On the contrary, the full sense of a hypocrite's heart is to please or promote himself. Though there may be some parentheses of religion, they are no part of the scope of his soul. You have their character in Psalm 78:36–37: "Nevertheless they did flatter Him with their mouth, and they lied unto Him with their tongues. For their heart was not right with Him, neither were they steadfast in His covenant." There is no greater sign of a rotten heart than a fundamental unsteadfastness in the covenant of God. When a man is ruled by times and companies to show good or evil, this man's heart is not right with God.

It's true, a tempest may bend the boughs of a living tree, or perhaps the tree itself if the storm is great, but they eventually return to their straightness. But the rotten sticks and branches are broken and overturned. Just so, some strong temptation may drive an upright man out of his honest way, but he soon returns and, by mending his pace, makes amends for his stumbling. Three Scriptures give the upright man his character concerning this matter.

Proverbs 28:14: "Happy is the man that feareth always." To be always afraid looks like a miserable life among men, but to have a waking eye and careful heart for fear of sin is no more a misery than to walk or ride with a vigilant regard to prevent a fall. This fear is not troublesome or vexatious at all; he is a happy man who uses it, and no wise man will account the other happy for going, running, riding without fear or wit in danger every moment to break his bones.

Hosea 12:6: "Keep mercy and judgment, and wait on thy God continually." The whole life of a sincere saint is a continual waiting upon God; whatever his work is, whoever his company might be, wherever he goes, whenever he eats or drinks, yet in all these he waits upon his God and serves the will of his heavenly Father.

Proverbs 23:17: "Be thou in the fear of the Lord all the day long." This is most emphatic for both the duty commanded and for the term of the duty; both are most appropriate to set out an upright man. The fear of the Lord is universal religion, so be in this. This is more than if he had said, "Let the fear of the Lord be in thee; be surrounded with it and swallowed up in it." And be in this all the day long, not only a fit of religion at your prayers in the morning and another at night, but work and walk, eat and drink in it all the day long, yea, all your life long, which is but a long day.

The religion of a hypocrite is like a tiring horse, which may go apace in the morning and show much mettle for a while; but the upright man, though more soberly, yet goes more constantly. And in this sense Proverbs 10:9 is most true: "He that walketh uprightly walketh surely." You shall find this man with savory thoughts in his heart at noon and with ejaculations to God at his work; there is a coherence between his duties and his life. In a word, the upright man has four "walks" towards God which will set him forth to the life.

1. The upright man walks *before* God. Genesis 17:1: "Walk before me, and be thou perfect," or upright. That is whereby the upright man habitually, always, and actually, as much as in him lies, sets the Lord always before him. The upright man thinks, speaks, and acts as if God looked on, weighing not only the matter, but the manner and motives of his ways, acquitting himself still to his God. 2 Corinthians 2:17: "As of sincerity, but as of God, in the sight of God speak we in Christ." Happy forever is that minister who can call God to record on his soul, that as no errors corrupt his doctrine so no base ends corrupt his heart; but that he

preaches Christ's will sincerely, as if the Lord Himself looked on.

2. The upright man walks *with* God, as did Enoch. Genesis 5:22: "And Enoch walked with God." That is so to live as if the Holy God were in person walking with you on earth, or as if you were walking with Him in heaven. If God should visibly walk with you on earth, as He was a while with Abraham, oh, with what humility, sanctity, watchfulness, love, and fear would you continually live? What a humble and serious regard would you have towards Him? Much more if you were to walk a while with Him in heaven, what a frame would you there be in? This sense of walking with God no man has skill in save the upright man; he is constantly religious.

3. The upright man walks *after* God. Deuteronomy 13:4: "Ye shall walk after the Lord your God, and fear Him, and keep His commandments, and obey His voice." Where he can see his God walk before him, like a dutiful child, he will walk after Him as fast as he can. The praise of Caleb in Numbers 14:24 was that he followed God fully. That simple declaration, "I am the Lord thy God," makes every "thou shalt" of His, and every "thou shalt not," acceptable to an upright man. "Come," says God, "here is a work I must have done. Here you must give, and here you must forgive; here is a saint who must be loved for his own sake, and here is a sinner you must love and pity for My sake." And the upright man says, "Lord, by Thy grace it shall be done." This is to follow God fully; and this is to walk after God.

4. The upright man walks *like* God. 1 John 2:6: "He that saith he abideth in Him ought himself also so to walk, even as He walked." Now how did our Lord Jesus walk when He was upon earth? Why, He was a mirror and pattern of all humility, justice, charity, meekness, and self-denial. Think often when you are eating, "How

did Christ order His meals? Do I give thanks like Him, discourse at the table like Him?" Think often when you are hearing and praying: "Did He hear and pray in such a manner as I do? How would He carry Himself among such neighbors? How would He instruct and guide this family? How would He bear and improve these reproaches, wants, and troubles? How would He appear for God in such company? How would He sanctify the Sabbath? How would He deal with such parents, such children, if He were in my place? How quiet would He be when provoked? How chaste would He be when tempted? How just and true would He be in His dealings, how cautious of others' names, and how content with His own estate?" Put Him often into your case and remember that, if ever you will live with Him, you must live like Him. By this fruitful and good life you show that God is upright, and that there is no unrighteousness in Him.

Section 10: The necessity of regeneration

And thus I have opened in some poor measure an upright heart. By all this, dearly beloved, you may see the absolute necessity of regeneration, I mean, the thorough change of the heart from the state of nature to the state of grace. For certainly man's heart by nature is false, and is far from this uprightness described. How can the soul receive Christ Jesus as He is offered in His gospel, or resign itself to Him, without regeneration? How can the heart of a sinful child of Adam be either single, sound, pure, perfect, or plain without regeneration? What man will study or practice inward, universal, and constant religion till he is regenerated? Who will walk before God, with God, after God, and like God before his heart is changed? Alas, these things are neither conceived by the mind nor received by the will of a natural man. He is ignorant in them and an enemy to them. Oh, you must be new creatures or else all our entreaties stand for nothing. We must still begin here, and can parley no further with you unless you yield in this. Will you be renewed in the spirit of your mind? Would you give all the world for a new heart? Till then you are but rotten at the heart; you walk in a vain show. For all your talk against hypocrites, you are errand hypocrites, and shall be condemned as such when those you have so reproached shall be your judges, and shall be openly honored before angels and men. Those poor Mordecais shall be royally arrayed, and you, like proud Haman, shall see it to the breaking of your hearts.

To prevent this, learn this one lesson, sound conversion, which is but restoring the image that you lost in Adam. Your bones were all put out of joint by the fall; this is the painful pluck that puts them in joint again. Would not any man abide a painful pluck to set one bone in joint? Oh, abide one pluck to bring all your soul into frame again. You must be new men or else you cannot be upright men; you must be in Christ before you can walk like Him. Your religion is but skin-deep till the Holy Ghost has made a holy change.

And therefore, for the Lord's sake, and for your soul's sake, study this point into practice. Give no sound sleep to your eyes while you are such near neighbors to hell; your temperate, just, and honest behavior may make you fall the softer, but without holiness you can never see the Lord—and a carnal heart can never be holy and upright without regeneration.

Section 11: The necessity of an upright life

Uprightness of life must accompany regeneration, or else it is but like a candle in a dark lantern which burns away to no purpose. This is the very sinew of human society and makes men happy in one another. It is such an excellent thing that they who never practice it

yet always pretend to it. The knaves abhor to be so
called, and would be reputed and called honest and upright men. And that must be amiable which all men
commend, and must be necessary which no society can
subsist without. So that there abides a crown of honor
for a downright heathen as well as a crown of glory for
an upright Christian; and there will be an easier pun-
ishment for those "christian pagans" than for the
abundance of our pagan Christians.

This uprightness of life is not sufficient without regeneration. It is good, but not good enough. To be a
fast friend to men and a broken bow to God will yield
you little comfort. Yet how many sit down here and
think themselves well? They would not steal a shoe
latchet from their neighbor for all the world, and yet
they make no conscience of stealing from God His
honor and His day. They would not wrong their
brethren's name by any reproach for all the world, and
yet they make no bones of wronging the name of the
great God, and take it in vain day by day. The square-
ness of your actions may crown you with reputation; but
the rottenness of your hearts will leave you in condem-
nation by that God who tries the hearts and reins. As in
the law, without blood there was no remission of sin, so
in the gospel, without oil there is no admission into
the kingdom of heaven. Civility and sanctity are two
separate things.

This uprightness of life cannot be without that uprightness of heart. It loses in truth its name and nature
for want of a principle. For that which is truly good
must have all its causes, which this lacks. It is a common experiment that water will not ascend above its
spring without a violence upon nature; and it is as true
that no man's actions can carry a higher level than the
fountain of them. So to make the life upright, you must
begin at the heart; first make the tree good, and then

the fruit will be good also.

Now this uprightness of life is the exact agreement of a man's words and actions with an honest and upright heart. Uprightness is when the life is the picture of the heart, and there is a blessed harmony betwen the frame of the soul within and the course of the life without; when a man does not frame his life to gratify the company or serve the times he lives in, or the corrupt humors of others, or any carnal ends of his own—but his heart is sincere, and so are his words and deeds. Not that we expect an absolute exactness here; the most upright man on earth has enough to humble and afflict him. But for the most part, there is no known ordinary and willing swerving of his course from his frame within, or of that from the holy will of God.

Section 12: A description of uprightness

The nature or being of uprightness of life shines in simplicity. Proverbs 28:6: "Better is the poor that walketh in his uprightness than he that is perverse in his ways, though he be rich." And Proverbs 28:18: "Whoso walketh uprightly shall be saved, but he that is perverse in his ways shall fall at once." The word for "ways" in both places is dual, and intimates two ways. A hypocrite is a man with two ways. One he goes in; the other he *seems* to go in. The poor, upright man has but one way, and that's better than them both. 2 Corinthians 1:12: "For our rejoicing is this, the testimony of our conscience, that in simplicity and godly sincerity, not with fleshly wisdom, but by the grace of God, we have had our conversation in the world." When this apostle was traduced by men, yet this afforded him not only content, but joy, to wit, the testimony of his conscience. A hypocrite may have quiet in his conscience, but an upright man has a testimony in his conscience. He carries everywhere testimonial letters in his bosom. And why all this joy? "That we have had our conversation in simplicity. As our ends have been single in preaching the gospel, so our lives have not been double. The drift of our preaching and lives has been the same." Happy is that preacher who can here subscribe his hand.

The simplicity of an upright man sometimes makes him the subject of loss and sometimes the object of scorn. Job 12:4: "The just, upright man is laughed to scorn." Many times he is called a simpleton, yet he goes on and carries it to the end. His great consideration is, "What is my duty?" Proverbs 4:25: "Let thine eyes look right on, and let thine eyelids look straight before thee." That is, without squinting at events, or how it will please, or whom it will lose; he is resolved to live and die in his duty. Do not misunderstand me. I am not saying that prudence and integrity cannot dwell together; certainly they may and ought to. His simplicity only excludes the subtlety of the fox, which stands in being cunning to do mischief, not the wisdom of the serpent, which stands in carefully avoiding it.

Uprightness of life also stands in purity. Proverbs 16:17: "The highway of the upright is to depart from evil." His usual road is as far from the broad way as he can have it be; and his care herein sometimes carries him rather too far, upon which account his conscience breeds more scruples than other men's, who can swallow anything that comes to pass. But his integrity in other things apologizes for him to all wise men, and at least brings him off with peace and comfort. And this very thing has brought upon very many of these upright men the badge of a "Puritan," which is by too many applied to subvert sincere holiness and to cast an odium on downright Christianity, and the practice of that we all profess. I am sure that the Scripture opens heaven's gates to none but those whose lives are pure and holy. Psalm 24:3–4: "Who shall ascend into the hill of the

Lord? Or who shall stand in His holy place? He that hath clean hands and a pure heart." Hence the upright man dares not mingle with those vain fooleries, vicious excesses, or suspicious recreations that men of devasted consciences are drowned in; nor can all the good nature that's in him, nor importunity of neighbors or kindred, draw him to such company or courses that would sting his conscience when he should sleep—unless God leaves him to himself sometimes to try to humble him.

This uprightness of life shines in the perfection of his life. I mean here a perfection of parts, in that each part of him is sincere. See Isaiah 33:14: "Fearfulness hath surprized the hypocrite. Who among us shall dwell with the devouring fire? Who among us shall dwell with everlasting burnings?" That is, who shall stand before the holy, just, and upright Jehovah? Who can approach Him when He executes judgments here or passes final sentance hereafter? When all hypocrites shall be in a fright, when their cobweb coverings shall fall off and they must stand naked (like so many cheats on a pillory) before God, angels, and men, who then shall stand with comfort and confidence? Mark verse 15: "He that walketh righteously [his feet walk uprightly] and speaketh uprightly [carries an upright tongue], he that despiseth the gain of oppressions [keeps an upright heart in him], that shaketh his hands from holding bribes [both his hands are upright too], that stoppeth his ears from hearing of blood [his ears are tipped with integrity], and shutteth his eyes from seeing evil [he looks with an upright eye]."

Thus you see he is upright all over. Let him deal with friends or enemies, with godly or ungodly, with wise or foolish; you may trust him, for he stands in awe of his God and of himself. He does not have one heart for his religion and another for his bargains and calling, but he studies the Scripture and drives his life into it as near as he can. This is to obey God's voice indeed. And from this perfection flows an excellent evenness of conversation, so that Queen Elizabeth's motto well becomes his life, "Always the same."

This uprightness shines in the plainness of his life. There are few criticisms in the life of an upright man. He's plain, and that's his prayer. Psalm 27:11: "Lord, lead me in a plain path"—that's my desire. He has no quirks, tricks, of legerdemain. If he cannot stand by plain dealing, he'll fall by it; when he trades and bargains, though he is discreet and careful, yet he is plain. When he reproves a fault or advises, he is sober, wise, and affectionate—but still he is plain. His discourse and sermons, though elaborate, yet still are plain. Among his very enemies, though he is cautious and considerate, yet there he is plain also. "Lead me in a plain path because of mine enemies." He is like him who wished his body were made of crystal so that his sincerity might be transparent.

Such was that martyr whom the persecutors required to reveal his companion whom they were prosecuting, promising to him his own life for the discovery; and so either by denying his knowledge of the place of his friend's abode or by betraying it, he might have saved his own life. After a little pause, he broke out into these words: "I cannot lie, and I will not betray him." So he laid down his life to save one of the brethren. Here was an upright man that would not tell a lie to save a life, who would rather die than lie. He will be plain, though he suffers for it. But how generally is this plainness banished out of the world? Most men walk in a vain show, disguising their intentions, looking one way and rowing another. The tropics are not more distant from England than most men's intentions are from their actions.

Section 13: The upright man is sincere in his words

The upright man is sincere in his words (Psalm 15:2). He walks uprightly and speaks the truth in his heart. His heart is indicting a good matter, and thereof his tongue is the pen of a ready writer. And indeed, that is the genuine use of words, to be the interpreters of the heart and mind. The upright man perhaps may not speak elegantly, but he can speak truly; he may not flourish his letters, but he can write a plain note; and his words you may believe more than others' oaths. These signs will set him out:

1. An upright man is a greater hater of flattery. He cannot abide to be either active or passive in it. He desires rather to know the worst of himself than to hear the best; for that open rebuke is better than secret love, and he knows that unjust praises are more dangerous than unjust slanders. And then for others, if he might get all the town by it, he cannot give flattering titles to any man or extol anything in anybody for his own ends. How fair an opportunity had Micaiah to have gained his liberty, and the favor of two potent kings, if he could have soothed Ahab in his vanity? But prison or no prison, he could not flatter. How easily might Paul have come off before Felix with a smooth oration if he had learned to have courted him and his Drusilla with a panegyric of praise? But he chose rather to speak of temperance, righteousness, and judgment to come to save them rather than soothe them in their sins.

It is true, he loses many a one by this plain dealing whom he might have kept by his flattery; but these are better lost than kept. Job 32:22: "I know not," said Elihu, "to give flattering titles; in so doing my Maker would soon take me away." These acts are below a man, much more below a Christian; and generally there is unsoundness in the heart or baseness in the ends of those

who use them. It is true, a man may, without any breach
in his uprightness, give another his due praises when
there is just occasion so to do; but to exceed bounds
herein, and that out of any base design of procuring
the same again, or for worldly profit, is very far from
true sincerity. A false heart and a flattering tongue usually go together. Proverbs 26:23: "Burning lips and a
wicked heart are like a potsherd covered with silver
dross." No man is so likely to have a double tongue as
he who has a double heart.

2. An upright man is a great hater of lying, a sin that
is directly contrary to the nature of sincerity. I may not
enlarge upon the kinds or aggravations of this sin;
whole sermons, yea, volumes are little enough to overthrow it, it is so common and so dangerous. If a lie will
save their credit, few will lose it; if a lie will gain anything, few will suffer loss; if a lie will shelter one from
another's anger, thousands will venture the displeasure
of the Eternal God before that of a silly worm, and
choose to have their head broken so that their helmet
may be spared. Oh, the woeful havoc of men's consciences by this sin!

Now an upright man abhors a lie; he knows that the
God of truth desires truth in the inward parts and has
in him a particular antipathy to this sin. Dress it in
what clothes you will, call it a jesting lie or an officious
lie, whatever lie you will—he does not like it and his
heart rises against it. Psalm 119:163: "I hate and abhor
lying," two words to show his great hatred of this sin.
Be it with him or against him, the upright man will
speak the truth.

Whereas a hypocrite, since he is nothing else but a
lie, so he can swallow them as fast as occasion serves.
Poor man! You would not speak it if the man who stood
by you saw into your heart. And how dare you speak it
when the holy and true God sees into your heart and

can choke you with your dissembling words?

3. An upright man hates all equivocations and mental reservations. That is, he speaks his words in the sense that he would have them construed in, and keeps no part of a sentence in his mind to contradict what he pronounced with his mouth, especially with an intent to injure another. Such was that juggling trick we read of Cydias, who, being trusted by Archetimus with a sum of money, afterwards flatly denied it. There being no witness to prove the truth, Cydias was summoned to his oath before the altar and a great assembly. He hid the money in his staff and, going to take his oath, gave Archetimus his staff to hold for a while. Then he confidently swore that he had given him back his money. But this deceit did not last long, for Archetimus, seeing his perjury, in a rage threw down his staff; it broke and the fraud was found. Such is the usual issue of such equivocations. The upright man has no skill at this; he knows if the plain truth will not bear him out, these cunning shifts never can. My brethren, it is unbecoming the plain-heartedness of a Christian to speak like the Delphian Oracle, to be understood in two contrary sentences.

The Romans themselves would not so much as hear those ambassadors who were painted, saying, "How shall we believe them whose very face and looks lie?" If an upright man does not speak all his heart, yet will speak according to his heart. He does not love to walk with a dark lantern, much less to deal with false lights; but plain and genuine are his expressions without, and fair and candid is his heart within.

4. An upright man greatly hates promise breaking, whether it is to God or men. A great note of integrity was in Jephthah. Judges 11:35: "I have opened my mouth to the Lord, and I cannot go back." It was a rash vow, but conscience of the obligation broke all other

considerations—which in his case might have been many—and he chose rather to have his very heart broken than his word. It is enough for a subtle politician to have distinctions and evasions ready to help himself out of the straightest bonds; the upright man does not delight after vows to make inquiry.

Well-advised every man should be before he binds himself in anything to the Lord; but when his soul is fast, let him be very well advised how he releases himself. Nothing more prostitutes the conscience, and nothing utterly undoes men more, than being fast and loose with God in sacred vows and promises.

The same abhorrence has the upright man of breaking his word with men; and thereupon his word is as good as his bond. If he bids so much for a commodity, he seldom shrinks but gives it; if he bargains to his prejudice, yet he does not change. The scarceness of the thing, the rising of the market, cannot prevail with him to rescind his punctual agreement; whether he gains or loses, he will not lose his honesty or his reputation.

Oh, what a golden age would return to us if men were but plain in their dealing and punctual in their performances? It is unworthy for a man, a Christian man, to be so vile that nobody can believe him or trust him. How will Atilius Regulus rise up in judgment and condemn this generation who—being prisoner at Carthage, and assured of his own death if he failed in his negotiation—was set at liberty to effect a peace at Rome upon the single security of his own word to return if he failed to procure it. But such was his public spirit that he effectually dissuaded his countrymen from a peace, assuring them of a certain conquest; and such was the integrity of his spirit that, after this, he fairly returned and accepted a cruel death rather than infringe his word. Ten thousand pities that such heroic acts should be lost for want of a right principle; and ten thousand shames that Christians should break their word for a coin while pagans will not do it for their lives.

Section 14: The upright man is sincere in his deeds

An upright man is sincere in his deeds or actions. Isaiah 33:15 says that he walks righteously as well as speaks uprightly. As his words are a true commentary upon his heart, so his actions are a true exposition upon his words. Whatsoever office or relation he stands in, he adorns it with integrity. When the upright judge puts on his robes, he puts off his worldly relations. The upright Justice of the Peace disdains to be drawn by favor or driven by fear from his duty. The upright counselor will not plead when his tongue is confuted by his conscience. The upright juror esteems the least grain of evidence more weighty than a talent of Ophir's gold. When the upright attorney perceives the cause to be a drop blown up by malice into a bubble, he sounds a retreat to his client, though he loses thereby. The upright physician will rather go with an empty purse than torture either the body or purse of his patient without cause. The upright tradesman will be upright in his words, upright in his weights, upright in his wares, and upright in his rates. And the upright minister will put on his Thummim, (that is, his uprightness, a word derived from that in my text) as well as Urim, and rather lose the love of ten by his plain dealing than the soul of one by dissimulation and unfaithfulness.

Thus uprightness, like a silver thread is drawn through the whole course of the sincere Christian. And he who is upright is upright everywhere.

To further set out this holy course, I will show what an upright man is most opposed to:

• An upright man is a great enemy to craftiness or

subtlety. Though he studies to be wise, yet he does not delight in cunning. Craft is wisdom degenerated; it is wisdom divested of honesty. A tang of this was in that practice of Rebecca's in Genesis 27:35 to procure the blessing for Jacob by her wiles. But it cost him many a sweating day and many a frosty night. Guile and guilt go hand in hand. Job 15:5: "Thy mouth uttereth thine iniquity, and thou choosest the tongue of the crafty." Carnal policy was never a friend to inward piety; though it sometimes wears lamb's wool without, yet it is always lined within with the fox's fur. But the true and holy God disappoints the devices of the crafty and drives the counsels of the froward headlong (Job 5:12). An upright man is clear in his thoughts and, though discreet, yet candid and fair in his dealings. And I doubt not to affirm there is no lawful calling under heaven but may be managed without this sinful craftiness. Away then with that idle pretense without which few tradesmen can subsist. Cursed is that trade that cannot stand without sin, said worthy Mr. [Richard] Capel. Better beg than sin; better starve than damn. Well fared the integrity of those noble Athenians who, in their war against the rest of Greece, were told by Themistocles that he had a strategy against their enemies, but it was not to be told publicly. So they wished him to tell it to Aristides. He told him it was to set the arsenal on fire where all the ships of the Grecians lay. Aristides then immediately told the people. His design was indeed profitable, but not just; and thereupon it was exploded by them all. Certainly the greatest wisdom in the world is to be a right honest man.

• An upright man is a great enemy to time-serving. There is a wise and faultless observing of the times. The men of Issachar, it would seem, were good at it (1 Chronicles 12:32). They had an understanding of the times so as to know what Israel ought to do. This is not only meant of weather-wisdom by rural observations, but also that by deduction from former times they could make directions for future times. And so Issachar is compared to an ass in Genesis 49:14 for the strength of his back, not the stupidity of his head. It is a point of great wisdom to know what to do, according to the will of God, in every turn of providence or change of condition, and in every company into which we come.

But there is a culpable temporizing, when a man has so mastered his conscience, and reduced it to that ready flexibleness, that for worldly ends he can think, speak, and act one way this day, this month, and this year, and then next day, next month, and next year another way. He can set his sails to every wind and please everybody to profit or preserve himself. He can turn, return, and overturn any turn to serve his own turn. And this temper is directly opposite to that uprightness we are describing. The upright man is deliberate in choosing and settling his principles, but a thousand worlds shall not alter him without clear evidence in his conscience. He is not a twining willow, but a sturdy oak; and whether the point he differs in is small or great, if it is a matter of conscience, though he will not be factious, troublesome, or uncharitable, yet all the rhetoric or rigor on earth will not remove an upright man from his course till God makes the business clear to his conscience.

How far the blast of temptation may for a time bend or bow a sincere Christian, or how long, no man can determine. The best are frail enough, and they who are most censorious of others' warpings would perhaps fall more foully if they lived under their temptations; but this base obsequiousness is no part of the man's uprightness. When the snare is broken, the sincere man will come to himself and there abide.

• An upright man is a great enemy to defrauding

others. He who studies that most righteous law (Matthew 7:12: "Whatsoever ye would that men should do to you, do ye even so to them), and has it written in his very heart, as that heathen emperor had it written in each room of his house, will abominate this most wretched practice. For which of you would be cheated or defrauded by another? Would you think it well to have a cracked estate offered to you; an unsound beast or unproveable wares imposed upon you; a blear-eyed Leah instead of a beautiful Rachel put upon you? You would condemn and dislike it.

Open the book of your own consciences; they will tell you that it is hateful therefore to deal so with another. The upright man considers that he is not born only to promote his own profit, that he should love his neighbor as himself, that all his bargains and doings in the world will be treed again, and therefore, let others do as they will, he will not do so because of the fear of God (Nehemiah 5:15). He is one who has laid this law upon himself: rather to suffer the greatest injury than to do the least injury, and that because he sees more evil in the least sin than in the greatest suffering. Besides that, he remembers and dreads that declaration from 1 Thessalonians 4:6, that no man go beyond or defraud his brother in any matter because the Lord is the avenger of all such. The conscience of his duty, and rooted liking of truth and equity, above all things steers him in these matters. He knows that there is as much honesty in stealing the money out of a man's purse, or robbing him by the way, as in willfully cheating or defrauding him; and therefore he will not do it in any matter.

That God who will put off His own worship till a man has undone his injury (Matthew 5:23–24) will never accept our most zealous service while we sleep with such unjust gain. Alas! Estates so raised are like the eagle's nest that was consumed with fire by the coal that came with the meat she stole from the altar. A fatal curse comes with such gain that at length destroys all the rest of a man's well-gotten goods. Now uprightness stands in a direct opposition to such indirect courses. He knows that he who has clean hands shall be stronger and stronger (Job 17:9) while, on the other side (to use a great statesman's proverb), frost and fraud shall both end in foul.

• An upright man (to finish the rough draft of this divine portrait) is an enemy to all manner of injustice, whether in respect of distributive or commutative righteousness. If the Lord places him in authority, he is the greatest hater of bribes and the least respecter of persons. Isaiah 33:15: "He shaketh his hands from holding of bribes," as if he were afraid to be burned in the hand with them. He will never revenge his private injury by public execution nor heed the merit of the person against the merit of the cause. It was said of Fabricius, that famous Roman, that one might as easily persuade the sun from its course as divert him from his upright and honest dealing. Such is our upright man in office: blind to faces, deaf to cries, and dead to threats and promises.

For commutative justice and dealing between man and man, you have his character already: he endeavors to exercise himself to have always a conscience void of offense towards all men (Acts 24:16). And so he raises an estate slowly, but he builds surely as he goes; and the generation of the upright after him shall be blessed.

And thus you see that his profession and his practice are the same. God helps him to spin an even thread throughout. He is the same in the camp below, for the main, as in the mount above; and there is a looking glass in his words and actions through which you may see his heart. It's true, this unbiased and steadfast course occasions him often much trouble in the world. He is called a singular, precise, and obstinate man by them who do not know him. Because he will humor none, he is often boxed in on both sides, and finds Livie's observation to be true: his impartial honesty neither finds friends nor abates his enemies. The most upright arbitrators please neither party. Yet, for all this, the comfort of his conscience feasts him; and before the scene is taken down he shall lose nothing by his integrity. Psalm 37:37: "Mark the perfect man, and behold the upright; for the end of that man is peace." Mark heedfully this man.

QUESTION. "Aye, but how can we know him? Uprightness is a character written out of man's sight and reading."

ANSWER. Why, thus: whereever you find a man's words and ways upright, you are bound to think that his heart is upright also. This is the law of charity; this is the law of equity. But what will be the end of him? "The end of that man is peace." He may meet with disquiets in his beginning and troubles in the middle, but "the end of that man is peace." Yea, there is no end of that man's peace. For that God who will not and cannot lie has said, "With the upright man will I show Myself upright."

And thus you see wherein stands the uprightness of a man.

Section 15: The scarcity of an upright man
And now, sirs, if all this makes an upright man, what shall I say! Where are these upright men? How very few is the number of them! The wise man was right right in Proverbs 20:6: "Most men will proclaim every one his own goodness; but a faithful man, who can find?" It is a general course for most men to blow their own trumpet. Most of their stories and discourses end

in themselves, and set out their own goodness; but a faithful, true, right man, who can find? The next verse will show him to you: He is "the just man walking in his integrity." That's the man in the Bible; now if we could just match him in the world.

I doubt not but there are many such in the world, but verily there are few such in comparison who are so resigned to God, resolved for God, such single-hearted, sound-hearted, sincere-hearted, whole-hearted, plain-hearted men; such inward, universal and constant Christians; persons of that simplicity, purity, perfection, and plainness of life and conduct; such enemies to flattery, lying, equivocation, promise-breaking, craftiness, time-serving, defrauding, and injustice. Good Lord! how rare are these on the earth in this Age. We have fallen into an age of atheists, scorners, brutes, and hypocrites; and we may sadly say with Micah 7:4: "The best of them is like a brier; the most upright is sharper than a thorn hedge." Innocent religion and sober piety is hooted out of the world; and upright men are derided who, if they were thoroughly known, would rather almost be adored.

My brethren, there are but few folks who bid likely for heaven, if this is an upright man. The judgment of charity is one thing, but when God's judgment of verity comes, the case will alter. Very, very few will hold weight by this balance, and as I need not, so I know not that I have made more ado than needs, or cut the way to heaven narrower than it is. It is reported of Pachomius, the famous Abbot among the ancients, that the 1300 monks he governed he divided according to the Greek letters into twenty-four classes or ranks, and sorted each to that letter that hinted his condition. For example, under *iota* the plain, single-hearted person, and under *pi* the close, intricate person. If we should rank Christians thus, how many would be crowded under the last letter, and how few under the first! And what need then do we have to mourn for the fewness of upright men, and to judge ourselves exactly lest we should be found to be none of them.

Chapter 2

The Uprightness of God

With an upright man, God will show Himself upright. This is evident for:

1. It is agreeable to His nature. Psalm 25:8: "Good and upright is the Lord." He is an upright God, and therefore loves uprightness. How can He choose, then, but to show Himself upright to an upright man? Simplicity, or a lack of duplicity, is God's first attribute, and simplicity is the upright man's chief property. There must therefore be a singular kindness between these two.

2. It is agreeable to His method. All divine and human stories show this to be His usual way. Witness Noah: he was upright in a rotten age, and the Lord was with him. Witness Abraham, who walked before Him and was upright, and God, though He was long in doing so, yet was sure in rewarding him. So with Caleb, so with Job, so with David, and so with all. No man can charge God with neglect or unfaithfulness towards him herein.

3. It is agreeable to His honor and interest. It is a prince's honor and interest to stick by his faithful and upright servants, or else he will quickly have none such about him. He would rather lose a world than lose his honor. And therefore in this psalm God will overturn the earth rather than leave upright David to his enemies. If fidelity and kindness will win him servants, Satan shall have but few. He can boldly implead all the world, much more his people: "O my people, what have I done unto thee? Testify against me" (Micah 6:3). He

would scorn to deal by his servants as Satan does, who drives them into a snare and there leaves them, who promises them a world and pays them with a hell.

4. It is agreeable to His promise. Psalm 97:11: "Light is sown for the righteous, and gladness for the upright in heart." However this seedness may be wet and sad, yet they shall have a joyful harvest. If any man on earth can lay claim to the promises, it is the upright man. What an unspeakable comfort it is to lay the finger of faith on any promise in the Bible and say confidently, "This is mine."

"Say no more, for I am weak and useless and sinful."

Yes, but are you upright? His Word is past, and there's an end. All the promises in this blessed Bible are in travail to be delivered into your heart. "To the upright man, He will show Himself upright."

God shows Himself upright with an upright man in the following ways:

Section 1: By overlooking his infirmities

This was Hezekiah's prayer at that famous passover in 2 Chronicles 30:18–20: "The good Lord pardon everyone who prepareth his heart to seek God, though he be not cleansed according to the purification of the sanctuary. And the Lord hearkened to Hezekiah." There were many who were really upright, yet not rightly and fully purified, as you may see in 2 Chronicles 29:34: "For the Levites were more upright in heart to sanctify themselves than the priests." Here were upright Levites, yet not sufficiently purified; but Hezekiah obtained for them a pardon of course for they had done what they could, and the Lord had mercy on them." This is a great comfort for ministers or people who, through straits of time or any unavoidable hindrance, are not rightly fitted and furnished for their respective duties and are afraid to come, and are even more afraid to stay away. The good Lord will pardon such a one. It was an oversight; the heart was sound at the bottom, and God will never break with any of His for an infirmity.

Compare Saul and David: Saul had foolishly (at most, covetously) spared Agag and a prey, and he was cast off for it and lost his kingdom. David defiled Bathsheba, killed her husband Uriah, and he was spared. He is, it is true, sorely beaten, but not turned out of doors.

Take Peter and Judas. Judas, through covetousness, betrayed his Master; and Peter, through fear, denied and foreswore Him. Judas was sent by the gallows into hell, and Peter was received into mercy. Why this different dealing? Why, David was, in the bent of his heart, upright before God, and Saul, in the bottom of his heart, was for himself. Peter resolved to lose his life before he would forsake his Savior, and Judas never followed Him but for the money. And therefore the Lord graciously pardons the unwilling infirmities of His people, for He sees the integrity of their hearts. A faithful husband is more satisfied with the bewailed failings of his poor wife than with the studied observances of an adulteress. And the Lord our God can better connive at and bear with the mourned-for infirmities of His dear children than with the feigned compliance of rotten hypocrites.

What a treasure of comfort is this for you who fear God! And let none else meddle with it! Your infirmities are many, and your fear is great, lest your infirmities should sink you forever. You have such raging passions, brutish lusts, frequent distractions, base distrust, unheavenliness of heart in ordinances, and dullness in them. These are your burdens, and these are your fears. Now all these are within the grant of pardon made in the covenant of grace; and you who are upright in heart, if any in the world have an undoubted interest therein, and so are forgiven in heaven, and will be forgiven in your consciences, so far as is good for you and shall be forgiven at the last day. You have God's Word for it in Psalm 32:1: "Blessed is he whose transgression is forgiven, whose sin is covered." But who is he who may claim this blessing? Verse 2: "In whose spirit there is no guile"; that is, an upright man, he who is no hypocrite. When therefore you have fallen into sin, do not sit poring and questioning your eternal state, but speedily and seriously set about the work of repentance and faith in the blood of Christ so that you may be made whole.

Indeed, after some great fall, or extraordinary fit of spiritual slumber, it is not amiss to clear and resettle the ground work (so far may the building be decayed that it may be easier to build anew than to repair the old). But it is neither wisdom nor duty upon every slip to condemn your state or to conclude that because you are wounded or sick therefore you are dead. Question your act, but not your state; condemn your acts of sin, but do not condemn your state of grace, nor brew more tears than you need to drink. For supposing you to be true men to God, resigned to Him, resolved for Him, and walking with Him to the extent of your power, He has graciously promised to pardon iniquity, transgression, and sin—sins of all sorts and sizes for them who fear Him and hope in His mercy.

And mark for your comfort that it belongs to God's truth and uprightness to pardon such a sinner. 1 John 1:9: "If we confess our sins, He is faithful and just to forgive us our sins, and to cleanse us from all unrighteousness." It is happy for us that we can plead mercy to God for pardon; but when we uprightly confess and forsake our sins, we may plead His justice and faithfulness. "O Lord, as Thou art just and faithful, bestow a pardon on me. I beg it in the uprightness of my heart; bestow it in the uprightness of Thy Word. For Thou hast said, 'With the upright man I will show Myself upright.' "

Section 2: By defending his person

The Lord will show Himself upright to an upright man by defending his person. He is made sometimes the butt of malice. Hell and earth conspire against him. Snares of death, floods of ungodly men, and the sorrows of hell are all bent against him. This is a clear argument of the sad degeneracy of mankind, to be so desperately set against the image of God in man, and to hate those who never did them wrong, and that for His sake who always does them good. Yet so is the case: the most innocent man cannot escape to heaven without many onsets; they bend their bow and lay snares, and can hardly sleep for rage. Wrongs and scorns, fines and prisons, are their usual charity; he who departs from evil ever makes himself a prey. The generality of the world is alienated from the life of God and are enemies in their minds to all who live it. Oh, that I could speak and write it in tears of grief and compassion! A drunkard, a swearer, and a whoremonger may live quietly with them. He who never reads the Scriptures, who never prays with his family, shall have all their good will, and go quietly by them into destruction; but if a man's conscience is once awakened, if he retrieves his course and falls to earnest prayer, changes his company and sinful courses, dares not profane the Sabbath or take God's name in vain, or swears as before, then all his neighbors rise up against him, watch him, censure him, malign him, and (if possible) ensnare him—while he (poor heart) thinks them no hurt, prays for them, and only strives to save his own soul and others if he can.

But here you may rest safely. 2 Samuel 22:31: "He is a buckler [shield] to all them that trust Him." The buckler covers the soldier, and God covers the upright man. They must shoot through God who will wound you to your hurt. They hit Him in the eye who aim at you; and they who will encounter Him best not meddle with their match. Exodus 19:4: "I bore you on eagles' wings." Other fowls bear their young in their claws so that the fowler may kill the young and the old one be safe; but the eagle carries her young on her wings so that whoever wounds the young must shoot through the mother. So does God carry His upright ones. God will suffer before they do; the Lord will suffer with them. Deuteronomy 32:11–12: "As the eagle. . .spreadeth abroad her wings, taketh them [her young] and beareth them on her wings. So the Lord. . . ." That is a sweet word in Psalm 7:10: "My defense is of God, which saveth the upright in heart." You may perhaps have no great friend to shelter you, no great estate to ransom you, but you have a great God to defend you, whose work and care it is to save the upright in heart. "I am thy shield," said God to Abraham. Fear not. If Omniscience is able to see and Omnipotence able to help, you are safe enough. And therefore, " 'Fear not, thou worm Jacob, and ye men of Israel. I will help thee,' saith the Lord" (Isaiah 41:14). A worm is a poor creature that few love and none fear. So are the seed of Jacob: they are persons that few love and none fear, and such as are most liable to dangers. Yet, says God, "Fear not, thou worm." A worm in the hand of God can withstand a world; and the gates (the utmost power and policy) of hell shall not prevail against one upright man. Proverbs 13:6: "Righteousness keepeth him that is upright in the way." His innocence is his shield. And the eyes of the Lord run to and fro throughout the whole earth, to show Himself strong on behalf of those whose heart is perfect towards Him. His all-seeing eye, His all-ruling providence, is employed in finding out all the designs of your enemies, to frustrate them or over-rule them, and to secure you whose hearts are perfect or upright before him. How secure would you be against a subject by such a word from a king? And may you not rest more on His Word, who is the King of kings? If you have His pass, you may go safe enough, even through armies of aliens.

Observable is that story told by Josephus of God's special providence. The Emperor Caligula commanded Petronius, his deputy in Judea, to set up his image in the temple. The Jews (ever since their captivity, keen against idolatry) begged and at length offered their necks and lives to him rather than admit such a profanation. Petronius pitied their condition and refused to execute his master's command. But the emperor was enraged, and sent his deputy a letter to slay himself, the usual doom of such persons. Caligula, however, shortly died, and his letter, meeting with some delay, was not brought unto Petronius till just after he had received the news of his death; and thus he escaped. Behold the admirable providence of God to those who stand upright.

Go forth therefore in your might; consider your duty and faithfully do it. Take no solicitous care what shall befall you. Do not study events, but study your work; not what man or devils will do, but what you ought to do; and not an hair of your head must fall to the ground. Wickedness proceeds from the wicked, but with the upright man He will show Himself upright.

Section 3: By strengthening his graces
The Lord will show Himself upright to this man by strengthening his graces and prospering him in his soul. His graces are weak, his bones are dried, and his soul is poor and needy. He pores for a whole week at times to find one plain piece of evidence of the grace of

God; but having an upright heart, and being a plant of God's planting, they shall increase and grow up as the calves of the stall. The child painted on the wall does not grow unless it is to grow more dim; but the child in the bosom, that has a principle of life, though it cries it grows; though it is sick yet sometimes it grows, and at length grows into a strong and virile man. So in this case, the painted hypocrite has no cubit added to his stature; no, he grows worse and worse. His varnish wears off, and nothing remains at length but a sepulchre without paint. But though an upright man groans, he grows; though he has some qualms, doubts, and troubles, yet he gains ground and (though insensibly) gathers strength.

It cannot be but that a sincere heart who is diligent in the means of grace must be changed from glory to glory. Micah 2:7: "Do not My words do good to him that walketh uprightly?" Certainly they do; he receives good though he perceives it not. A living man who eats heartily must gather strength unless he has some predominant disease—though perhaps he does not perceive renewed strength at every meal. So an upright man, being truly alive to God through Jesus Christ and careful in the use of all God's ordinances, must increase his spiritual strength though perhaps he sees no present profit by this prayer or that sermon, unless he lies under the tyranny of some imperious sin for a time. Proverbs 10:29: "The way of the Lord is strength to the upright," which most properly signifies that religion secures an upright man. The ways of God and godliness are strength, and bring strength to the upright. He who is planted in the house of the Lord shall still bring forth fruit (Psalm 92:13–14). It is one thing to be placed in the house of the Lord. Many a carnal gospeller has a seat there, and appears there from one year's end to another; but it is another thing to be planted there, to

have a root of knowledge, repentance, and uprightness—and such must grow and go from strength to
strength.

Do not be therefore discouraged, O you of upright
hearts, for your grain of mustard-seed will become a
tree. Though your graces seem weak, they shall be
strong. "To him that hath shall be given, and he shall
have abundance." You have a little faith and love, aye,
but God has said that you shall have abundance. Do not
despise the day of small things. Ply your oars, for the
ship is passing though you think it stands still, and you
will be at the shore ere you are aware. Ephesians 6:24:
"Grace be with all them that love our Lord Jesus Christ
in sincerity." Here's a blessing that reaches even you.
Grace, all grace, of all sorts and sizes, be with you,
though it does not appear to you in all ages of the
church and in all places of the world, who love our
Lord Jesus Christ. Perhaps you cannot preach for
Christ, write, consult, nor fight for Christ. No, but you
can love Jesus Christ. You can love Him as a Lord to
rule you, as a Jesus to save you, and as a Christ to teach
you. Why, here is grace in the promise, in the blessing
for you. But Christ must be loved in sincerity: Jesus
Christ Himself, and Jesus Christ for Himself. And then
be assured that grace shall be multiplied to such a soul.
As it is God's judicial method, when men are resolved
to go on in sin, to give them up (Revelation 22:11: "He
that is filthy, let him be filthy still"); so, when a man is
uprightly bent to serve Him, He spurs him on with His
Word and Spirit, saying, "He who is righteous, let him
be righteous still." And thus herein to the upright man
He shows Himself upright.

Section 4: By hearing his prayers

The Lord shows Himself upright to the upright
man by hearing his prayers. Proverbs 15:8: "The sacri-

fice of the wicked is an abomination to the Lord, but the prayer of the upright is His delight." No music is so sweet to men as sincere prayers are to God. The upright man delights to pray, and the upright God delights to hear. How pleasant is the child's first language to the father? He would rather hear it than an elegant oration; and the reason is, first, it is his own child, and, second, it speaks (poor thing) as it thinks. There is no color upon its words nor dissimulation in them. Even so the prayers of the upright man are most welcome to God, his heavenly Father, for the child is His own, and his prayer is the content of his heart. He cries against his sin, and also he hates it; he sues for grace, and he heartily longs and endeavors for it. Hearts can come into heaven when words must stand at the door. God gets out of the hearing of many a starched oration, but He gets nigh to those who call upon Him in truth (Psalm 145:18). Oh, when confessions are the sad note of a bleeding heart, when supplications are the real breath of an hungry soul, the Lord listens to such melody.

There is a vast difference between the formal note of a young beggar and the sensible cries of him who is half-starved. We neglect the former and are ready to serve him only with reproof; but when the other cries who begs in truth, his face cries, his rags cry, his tears cry, the whole beggar cries, and then we draw out our heart and hand unto him. Even so our gracious God slights and hates affected words that come from an un-affected heart; but when the heart comes up with them, then He comes and brings His alms with Him and His reward before Him. Oh, what encouragement should this give to an upright-heart! You have an ear for God, and He has an ear for you. You are ready and quick in your obedience, and He is as quick and ready in His audience; you are punctual to yield to Him in anything, and He is punctual to yield in anything unto you. In a word, you are resolved to do His will, and He is resolved to do yours. Hence Luther boldly said, "Let my will be done, because it is Thine." Yours are broken prayers, but they are upright prayers. There may be no rhetoric in them, but there is logic in them, arguments that will conquer God Himself. There is no argument on earth like integrity, nor in heaven like the blood of Christ.

OBJECTION. "Ah, but then I fear my state and doubt my sincerity, in that I have prayed long for such a child, for a better memory, for strength against some sins, and have received no answer. So I may conclude myself a very hypocrite."

ANSWER 1. God often delights in prayer when He seems to deny it and never denies His servants but when denying is better than granting. You must distinguish between delaying and denying: our God delays to try us, not to deny us, to make us cry the louder; so He put off Jacob to whet him all the more. He seemed to be weary of his company, but he would not pass so; God made him lame, yet Jacob prayed and wrestled on one leg rather than give up. So it was with the woman of Canaan. Drink is more welcome when we are very thirsty; and when the Lord sees you cannot be without a mercy, you shall have it. And then the greatness of the mercy shall pay for the length of its stay; and, like money earning interest, so your prayers, which have been long on file, shall bring the greater increase back again.

ANSWER 2. God often hears our prayers when we do not perceive it. In this sense, He speaks once and twice, yet man perceives it not. Psalm 138:3: "In the day when I cried, Thou answeredst me, and strengthenedst me with strength in my soul." On the same day that his letter was sent, he had an answer. And what was it? Why, he was strengthened with strength in his soul. If he

were not answered in the letter, yet he was answered in
the better. God often gives gold when we ask for silver.
God denied Abraham regarding Ishmael, but He gave
him Isaac. He denied Moses Canaan, but gave him
heaven.

Sometimes our thirst for more makes us think we
have received none. Rich, covetous people never have
enough because their desires are insatiable. When you
arrive at heaven, you shall see that the Lord booked every petition and answered it in the best manner for you.
It may be that you are denied for one child, but God
gives it to you in another; or perhaps the grandchild
reaps the prayers that you sowed for the father. The
Lord may not give you a stronger memory, but may bestow on you a softer heart. You discern no strength
against some sins, yet you have deeper throws of repentance for them. Still it is an inviolable truth that the
upright man's prayer, when it is put up in Christ's
name for things that are agreeable to God's will, is graciously heard and answered in mercy.

Do not therefore let your Father's seeming denials
trouble you; for our wise God sometimes yields to the
suits of Satan himself, while He demurs upon the supplications of His own servants. (Compare Job 2:5 and
Luke 8:32 with Genesis 17:18 and Matthew 26:39.) But
then His grants to Satan are for his greater confusion,
and His denials to His children are for their greater
consolation.

Section 5: By comforting him in his troubles

The Lord shows Himself upright to the upright
man by comforting him in his troubles. Psalm 116:6:
"The Lord preserveth the simple [that is, the upright]. I
was brought low, and He helped me." His integrity does
not free him from the common infirmities of mankind, such as wants, sickness, prisons, losses, crosses,

unkindnesses, and death itself at last; but his God takes special care to support and comfort him and, at length, to deliver him. In all these storms he is sure of sunshine, and the sunbeams guild every drop that the clouds pour down and make the storm as a calm. So the face and favor of God refreshes the upright in heart, for Psalm 11:7 says, "The righteous Lord loveth righteousness. His countenance doth behold the upright." And unworthy is that man of heaven's glory who does not prefer the sharpest sickness, the darkest prison, or the heaviest cross with the light of God's countenance, before the riches of Egypt with His frowns.

This made Paul and Silas sing in prison while Felix trembled on the throne. And they say that the Apostle James was so cheerful at his martyrdom that one who drew him to the tribunal was converted by it. For death, that king of terrors that dismounts the proudest spirits, the most effectual refuter of all atheists and surpriser of hypocrites, is disarmed of all its terribleness by an upright heart. Isaiah 57:2: "He shall enter into peace; they shall rest in their beds, each one walking in his uprightness." The bed of a hypocrite is a grave wherein he lies rotting in his sins; the grave of an upright man is a bed of spices wherein his body is at rest, whose soul has walked before God in uprightness.

Oh, be of good cheer, then, all you single-hearted ones. The handkerchief of God's love shall wipe away your tears, and His potions shall prevent your faintings. The lions shall roar, and the young lions suffer hunger, but they who fear the Lord shall not want any good thing. If wants are good for you, look for them; if sickness is good for you, be content with it; if prisons, if losses, if crosses come, they shall do you no hurt. Every stream of providence, however fierce, is channeled through that promise that all things shall work together for good to them who love God. His properties,

His promises, and His providences all smile on the
true-hearted man. Poor men, your straits may be great;
poor women, your pangs may be sharp; but all is for
good, yea, for the best. God is with you, the great, wise,
and holy God. And is this nothing? Are the consola-
tions of God small to you? If He gives quietness, who
then can make trouble? Heaviness may endure for a
night, but joy comes in the morning. The story always
ends well for the sincere-hearted man. Psalm 112:4:
"Unto the upright there ariseth light in the darkness."
Dark providences may well be borne when clear
promises are sealed upon the heart. This was noble
Hezekiah's comfort, when all forsook him. Isaiah 38:3:
"Remember now, O Lord, I beseech Thee, how I have
walked before Thee in truth, and with a perfect heart."
In other words, "I have done uprightly with Thee; now
deal uprightly with me; now remember." The Lord has
too good a memory to forget such a man in his needs.
He gave him a lease gratis of fifteen years on both his
life and his kingdom.

Who would not entirely love and serve such a God?
He is the poor man's Friend, the sick man's Doctor,
yea, and Bedmaker, the prisoner's Companion. The
true-hearted, the unwearied, the everlasting God is a
very present help in trouble. Name the strait wherein
God has not supported or relieved His people. Ask your
fathers, and they shall tell you how in six troubles and
in seven He has been with them. All the patriarchs can
prove this: Abraham, Job, and Daniel. Speak only with
David: was he not very poor when he sent to crave of
Nabal? God gave him contentment and, at last, plenty.
Was he not in dreadful hazard in Keilah, in Gath, and
in Mahanaim? Yet he came off well and died in his own
bed. Was he not for a time so very sick that some said
that an evil disease clung to him? Yet God remembered
him and made him safe and sound.

All the saints will bear witness that God is no flincher of His friends. Yea, at last all men shall say with Psalm 58:11: "Verily there is a reward for the righteous; verily He is a God that judgeth in the earth." Though things seem to go cross with His poor children, yet, take one thing with another; and He deals very uprightly with them. "In very faithfulness Thou hast afflicted me." If they want a fuller table, yet they have a lighter heart; if they have not such costly clothes, yet they have more healthful constitutions; if they do not reach such vast treasures, yet they can enjoy the light of God's countenance, which is far better.

Artabazus thought himself wronged when Cyrus gave him a golden cup at a feast and to Chrysantas only a kiss of respect, deeming thereby that he had a lesser portion of kindness than the other man. And shall we not much more value His glorious smiles above the greatest earthly gifts? "Let Him kiss me with the kisses of His mouth, for His love is better than wine." Though you are not delivered from your straits, yet, being upheld in them, you are well. It was all one to Daniel and his friends to be kept in the fire as to be kept out of it. One way or another, light shall spring to the righteous and joy to the upright in heart.

Section 6: By directing him in his doubts

The Lord shows Himself upright to the upright man by directing him in his doubts. Proverbs 11:3: "The integrity of the upright shall guide them." Many an upright man is under great doubts and does not know what to believe or what to do. Arguments and pleas on both sides, great men on one side and good men on another (for seldom are they both on a side), likely reasons court his assent either way. The commands of men are sometimes countermanded by his conscience, and he wants parts, learning, and judgment to split

hairs and state the case exactly, either of faith or fact.
Now in this case, when a man has used the means of
resolution that he is capable of, the integrity of the upright shall guide him. His plain, honest heart is neither suspicious of more evil to be in men or things
than evidently appears; nor, on the other side, does he
study extricating salvos or subtle evasions to sleep with
a whole skin and salute the upper party. But, according
to his best knowledge, he fixes his faith and orders his
actions by the rule of God's Word, which he knows will
best bear him out.

An upright man sometimes meets with doubts in
matters of faith, but herein he stands fairest for that
promise which Christ has made to lead him into all
truth. Though his integrity may not secure him from
error, yet it will secure him from being a heretic.

He has doubts sometimes about things to be done
towards God in his worship and towards men in his
life. In the former, he studies the will of God in His
Word, knowing that nothing which is offered to Him
will please Him unless it is directed by Him. As for
men, he is relieved in most of his doubts by that golden
rule found in Matthew 7:12: "Whatsoever ye would that
men should do to you, do ye even so to them."

Last, he is perplexed with some doubts about the
love of God and the salvation of his soul. But here also
his integrity so guides him that he is far from presum-
ing, though he is loath to despair; and the Lord gives
him comfort because of his sincerity, though he may
lack the joy from assurance. And is not uprightness a
choice jewel to lay claim to this guidance? Psalm 25:8:
"Good and upright is the Lord; therefore will He teach
sinners in the way." This conducting a poor sinner in
the way flows from His goodness and uprightness; and
therefore, as long as there is a drop of goodness or a
dram of uprightness in God, the penitent sinner shall

never lack a guide. And to this refers that promise in Isaiah 30:21: "Thine ears shall hear a word behind thee saying, 'This is the way; walk ye in it, when ye turn to the right hand, and when ye turn to the left.' " Some think this alludes to a schoolmaster prompting his scholar over the shoulder how he should pronounce his words when he (poor child) is puzzled and does not know not what to say. Even so will God lead His upright ones in the way that they shall choose when they are in the dark. You shall find Proverbs 13:6 to be true: "Righteousness keepeth him that is upright in the way. but wickedness overthroweth the sinner."

Resolve then in such cases, after you have used the means of illumination, as Jehoshaphat in another case, "O Lord, I know not what to do, but mine eyes are unto Thee." That is, "I perceive the blindness of my eyes, but Thou seest the uprightness of my heart. I would do Thy will if I knew it. Teach me Thy way, and I will walk in Thy truth; consider my weakness, and neither leave me in perplexing doubts nor suffer me to err from Thy will." Be sure that God will not forsake you, for it is plain that many an honest heart is preserved in the way of truth when many of great but unsanctified parts have fallen into damning errors. With the upright man, God is used to showing Himself upright.

Section 7: By vindicating his integrity

God's uprightness to the upright man will yet appear by clearing his integrity. Sincerity has the sweetest visage, but bad men put on it often the foulest vizard; and many a dear saint wears the note of a hypocrite to his grave. Though no man is as far from hypocrisy as this man, no sin he hates more; yet this character is usually fastened on our plain-hearted man.

It is the subtlety of Satan to charge the saints with those sins whereof he is sure they can hardly clear

themselves till the day of judgment. And those are
commonly these two: covetousness and hypocrisy, both
of which, for the nature of them, lie so within that it is
almost impossible to repel his charge. Hence the apostle is driven in the former to make his appeal to God in
1 Thessalonians 2:5: "For neither at any time used we
flattering words, as ye know [for this you can clear us],
nor a cloak of covetousness, God is witness [herein God
only can purge us]." And the like is said in Romans 1:9:
"For God is my witness, whom I serve with my spirit."
The upright Lord will clear up these men's integrity,
first or last.

Holy David lay under many heavy charges, and that
for a long time. "How long will ye turn my glory into
shame?" His critics said that he was not fit to live in his
own native country, that he hatched treason against
Saul and undermined his government, and that he had
no religion; but at length his righteousness shone as
the noonday; Saul himself was convinced of David's integrity and acquitted him, though thereby he condemned himself. Upright Job passed for a notorious
hypocrite among his enemies, for he was accounted no
other by his friends; but the Lord brought out his justice as a lamp that burns.

What is more common in the world than to brand
everyone as a hypocrite who is serious in his religion? If
any man humbly and conscientiously endeavors to live
according to his baptismal covenant—to set himself
against the world, the flesh, and the devil, and deny the
pomps and vanities wherein the generality of men wal-
low—presently his envious and carnal neighbors, when
they can tax him with nothing, condemn him as a hypocrite. His outside is smooth, but inwardly he is a
downright hypocrite, they say. But his upright God,
who knows his heart, will clear him sooner or later—at
furthest at that great day of setting things at right. The

Lord Jesus will come with His thousands of saints (Jude 14–15) to convince the ungodly world of all their hard speeches, which ungodly sinners have spoken against him: "See here, you implacable wretches. This is the man, this is the woman, whom you condemned as a hypocrite; they were praying for you while you were cursing them. I knew their uprightness and will now declare it. Thus shall it be done to those I delight to honor, and you must go with a curse into eternal torments."

Rejoice in the Lord, therefore, O you righteous; and be glad, all you of upright heart. Do not be dismayed at men's rebukes; these reproaches only add to your crown. And God permits them to make you search your hearts all the more. Though these are poor commodities, yet you may make a trade of them and live the better for them. They charge you with the fox's pranks, and you have the fox's nature. They charge you with one fault, and thereby you find out another; they write "hypocrite," and you subscribe to being "formal, dead, secure, and chief of sinners."

And know for your comfort that your names shall have a resurrection as well as your bodies; and you shall shine in glory while your enemies shall only shine in flames. Even in this world your God justifies you in their consciences; most of them would wish their souls in your soul's stead, for all their talk. When pale death stares them in the face, then they will cry out, "O, let me die the death of the righteous, and let my latter end be like this." It is not often that a hypocrite goes undiscovered to his grave, nor very often that an upright man dies without the testimony of the centurion, even from men, "Certainly this man was a dear child of God!"

Section 8: By preserving him to the end
The Lord shows Himself an upright God to the up-

right man by preserving him to the end. It is elementary fire that goes out; the celestial ever burns. Proverbs 10:29: "The way of the Lord is strength to the upright." The upright man alone is the persevering man. The fixed stars appear but small; the blazing Star looks far greater. But the former abide from age to age; and the latter, being but exhalations compounded of corruptible matter, are spent and consumed to nothing. They had, perhaps, more eyes fixed on them than on the others, but they waste away. Even so a hypocrite may make a greater blaze in his profession, may be more admired and talked of in the world, but the real saint is fixed; he abides, no tempest can shake him; he is built on a Rock and abides forever.

The way of the Lord is strength to the upright. Every prayer strengthens him; every sermon strengthens him; yea, every temptation (like the wind to a well-rooted tree) causes his roots to spread and stand stronger. He may be moved, but not removed; he may fall, but not fall away. An upright tree does not fall as soon as one that leans. An upright man never makes a downright apostate. Psalm 25:21: "Let integrity and uprightness preserve me; for I wait on Thee." Those are two good props to a weak Christian. He may still say, "Lord, I have but weak graces to preserve me. I have no parts or learning, and I have few friends to hold me up in Thy ways. But I have (Thou knowest) a sincere desire to please and serve Thee. Oh, let integrity and uprightness preserve me, and for those I wait on Thee. I wait in the use of the means of perseverance, and I wait by faith upon Thy promise. If sincerity will not hold me up, I must fall."

He who walks in a narrow way must not reel; if he reels, he is in danger of falling. The true Christian goes in such a way that leaning is next to falling. The upright man walks uprightly, and therefore surely. He has lived to see great scholars, great professors, and great preachers dwindle to nothing, but by grace he stands.

This is a great comfort and security to a poor soul. "My stick is small, yet I hope I shall never break. I drive but a mean trade, but I perceive that I do not go backwards. It is better for me to be a lowly saint than a great hypocrite. My heart is sound. I have no secret reserves. I know nothing by myself. I cannot run as fast as others, but I am on the way that will certainly bring me to God's holy hill. Job 27:5–6: "Till I die, I will not remove mine integrity from me. My righteousness I hold fast; my heart shall not reproach me as long as I live."

Among the many needless fears of the servants of God, this is one that disquiets the soul when God stands by only looking on, namely, "Shall I hold out? I am a very weak creature, and the fall of one tree shakes another. I have seen great cedars fall; they were once as confident as I. If trials come, what will become of me?"

Study and believe that excellent Scripture in Jeremiah 32:40: "I will make an everlasting covenant with them, that I will not turn away from them to do them good." Make a stand here poor soul. The eternal true and upright God has entered with you, even with the weakest and youngest believer, into an everlasting covenant that, for His part, notwithstanding all your infirmities, He will never (mark), never turn away from doing your soul good.

"Oh, but my fear is," says many an upright heart, "that I shall forsake Him, and turn from Him. That is my fear."

Then mark what follows: "And I will put My fear in their hearts, that they shall not depart from Me." So then as God will not turn from you, so you shall not depart from Him. How then could you fall away! And all this is in His everlasting covenant that cannot be disannulled.

When therefore your fears come cold upon your hearts concerning your perseverance, plead this Scripture with God. Fasten it on your souls. Do not fear falling off with a fear of diffidence. You are allowed a fear of caution, for that will make you stand the faster; but beware of a fear of diffidence, for that will make you fall the sooner. Look to the rise, root, and beginning of your religion, and God will look to the end of it. Though your grace was but like a grain of mustard seed, yet it shall be come a great tree. Job 8:6–7: "If thou wert pure and upright . . . though thy beginning was small, yet thy latter end shall greatly increase." He who has taken root in Christ can never wholly wither.

Section 9: By bestowing outward blessings on him
God will show Himself upright to the upright man by bestowing outward blessings upon him. Proverbs 28:20: "A faithful man shall abound with blessings." To these he can make the clearest claim; of these he has the truest tenure. They shall always be provided for his good. Proverbs 14:11: "The house of the wicked shall be overthrown, but the tabernacle of the upright shall flourish." The eyes of the Lord are upon him and his house to do him good from the beginning of the year to the end of the year. Health, wealth, peace, and full contentment shall be heaped on him so far as they are good for him. That upright Caleb, whose title of honor it was that he followed God fully (Numbers 14:24), had a double portion (so the learned say) in the land of Canaan.

He who has the sovereignty over the world, and all that is therein, loves the upright; and he who loves gives liberally. Proverbs 15:6: "In the house of the righteous is much treasure." We count our friends among our treasures. Every loaf of bread, every shilling in his purse, every corn, yea, every pile of grass in the field is a friend's token to the upright man, so that in his house there is a world of treasure. The upright God (in effect) says to His angels every day, "Recommend to Me such a child this morning, and carry to him from Me his daily bread, this or that mercy that is good for him." Hence we have that ample promise in Psalm 84:11: "For the Lord God is a sun and shield; the Lord will give grace and glory. No good thing will He withhold from them that walk uprightly."

Oh, blessed promise! Do you want direction? He is a sun. Do you want protection? He is a shield. Do you want grace? He will give grace. Would you have glory? He will give that also. Have you need of other good things for your comfort in this life? No good thing will He withhold from those who walk uprightly.

Now, sit down and think what you can wish for or need that is not here promised. And this all comes from that God who cannot deceive, and who is able and resolved to make good on His word. Put all the worldling's lands, palaces, bonds, and bags into one scale, and this one verse on the other, and see which one will weigh the most. You will quickly discern that they are lighter than vanity, and this one verse of more weight than the whole world. Rest your weary hearts in this: "If health were good for me, I know I would have it; if riches were good for me, I would have them. For I have my upright God in a bond that He will withhold no good thing from me."

Yet further, see Psalm 112:2–3: "The generation of the upright shall be blessed. Wealth and riches shall be in his house, and his righteousness endureth forever." Your great care and fear is for your posterity; lo, here's a promise for them also: "The generation of the upright shall be blessed." Though we cannot certainly be assured of this to every upright man's child, yet this promise gives the upright man more ground of hope than any hypocrite or wicked man in the world can have.

There is a stock of your prayers going in heaven, and there is a stock of God's promises in the Bible. Why then should you distrust? Sooner or later your posterity will certainly reap them, either in temporal or spiritual mercies. God may be long, but He will be sure. The covenant is made with you and yours, and the generation to come shall fare the better for your integrity. Abraham hardly enjoyed one foot of that land which fell to him for his true-heartedness, but his posterity had it all. And many an upright man lives and dies but with an ordinary estate, for he dares not do wrong to grow rich; but the Lord remembers his posterity, and his seed shall be mighty in the earth. "The generation of the upright shall be blessed."

Hold on, therefore, to your integrity; you are on the way of preferment. Proverbs 21:21: "He that followeth after righteousness and mercy findeth life, righteousness, and honor." He finds more than he looked for. It is true, the vilest men may be exalted, and the posterity of evil men may be both great and good; but they have no such promise for it as you have. They may have fairer houses, finer fare, and costlier clothing; but they have a curse with it, and a sad reckoning to come. Oh, therefore, for your health's sake, for your estate's sake, for your posterity's sake, but above all for your soul's sake, for an upright God's sake, study integrity. Be true-hearted, sincere-hearted, and whole-hearted men for God.

Section 10: By crowning his integrity

God will show Himself upright to His upright ones by crowning their integrity with internal peace. Melchizedek was first the king of righteousness and then King of Salem, king of peace. And where Christ has engraven sincerity, which is the true righteousness, then follows peace and joy in the Holy Ghost. There's no rest but in religion, nor any sound peace but in piety. Others may have quiet of conscience, but the upright man has the testimony of his conscience, and that is quite another thing. Theirs is but a truce, and a day's sickness will break it. The hypocrite has a pacified conscience, but what is this without a purified conscience? It is righteousness and peace that alone will kiss each other.

The quiet of most men's consciences is from their blindness, not from their goodness. Thus the beasts are well because they know no better and fear no worse. Thus millions lie still and die like lambs. If these had more knowledge, they would have less quiet. They are like the malefactor in a dungeon who does not see his misery, or as the bird who is busy at the chaff and does not see the net. One thundering threat set on by the spirit of bondage will spoil all their mirth.

There can be no true peace where sin is suffered in quiet. It would be well for such as you to be frightened. Cries would be your best music, and tears the best nectar you could drink. You must be allowed to bleed or die; such is your disease that you must be lanced or lost. But now, when true grace comes in, after that spiritual conflict that breaks the heart of sin, the conscience has a sweet peace, or at least ground for it. The law charges, the devil charges, but conscience in Christ's blood discharges. He who makes conscience of sin has his conscience free from sin. Now I can eat and sleep and go in the dark; my conscience bears me witness in the Holy Ghost, though the earth is removed and the mountains are carried into the midst of the sea—yet here's tranquility. "In the world ye shall have tribulation, but in Me," said Christ, "ye shall have peace." And this is the fruit of uprightness. Isaiah 32:17: "And the work of righteousness shall be peace; and the effect of righteousness, quietness and assurance forever." While Francis Spira kept on in his upright way, he had a heaven of peace; but after his sinful compliance, he did not have one day or hour of quiet in his soul. Sincerity and serenity live and die together.

God also crowns the upright man's integrity with eternal glory. There He pays the upright man for all. When his God leads him into the land of uprightness (Psalm 143:10), there he shall meet with all God's hidden ones, of whom the world was not worthy. Ah, poor hypocrite! He does not know what to do when he dies; each step he takes is towards hell. The longer he lives, the nearer is his destruction. Job 27:8: "For what is the hope of the hypocrite, though he hath gained [wealth, reputation, etc.], when God taketh away his soul?" Their very hope, which is all the comfort that is left them, will flee away and leave them in the briars. But then the upright man shall be somebody. Here he is a prince unknown; there he enters his kingdom. Here he is under a cloud; there the righteous shall shine as the sun forever and ever. He who has an estate in reversion, though he lives poor for a while, yet the estate will fall to him at last. And the upright man's inheritance is uncorruptible and undefiled; it does not fade away. And this as sure as God is in heaven. Genesis 15:1: "Walk before Me, and be thou perfect. I will be thy exceeding great reward." Who can desire more than Him who is all?

It will be merry when the upright God and the upright man meet. "Are you he who received My dear Son, and resigned your heart so freely to Him? Are you he who gave inward, universal, and constant obedience to My will? Are you he who stuck to Me in such and such times and trials? Are you he who walked righteously and spoke the truth in your heart? Come up here!

Angels, put on his crown. Sing an anthem, you sons of
the morning, at My upright servant's coming home!
Come, enter into the joy of the Lord. Here live and love
and rejoice forever."

Psalm 140:13: "Surely, the righteous shall give
thanks unto Thy name; the upright shall dwell in Thy
presence." Now many a poor upright heart has barely a
house to cover his head, scarcely a bed to rest on. He
may not dwell here or there. But there is but one breath
between him and a glorious palace, where the spangled
firmament is but the floor. He has a house paved with
rubies and filled with saints and angels, like so many
suns; and there he shall dwell and sing among them,
world without end. Into that corporation all upright
men may come, and their greatest enemies will never
follow them. Seeming saints will be in the church, but
none but sincere saints may come into heaven.
Matthew 5:8: "Blessed are the pure in heart, for they
shall see God."

Rejoice therefore in the Lord, O you righteous; and
shout for joy, all you who are upright in heart! Oh, what
a shout there will be in heaven when all this blessed
tribe meet together and have Christ among them! And
then you shall see how the righteous Lord loves righteousness, and how His countenance beholds the upright. Then you shall be paid for every drop of blood,
for every drop of tears, for every step, for every thought
that you have laid out for His name.

Chapter 3

The Application

What may we gather hence for the bettering of our minds or manners, to inform the former and reform the latter?

Use of Information

This doctrine proclaims the equity of God. To an upright man God will show Himself upright. Why, then, His ways are equitable. "Though clouds and darkness be round about Him [though His ways are hidden], yet righteousness and judgment are the habitation of His throne [they are always holy, just, and equitable]" (Psalm 97:2). He who has a cause to be tried regarding land or life counts it a privilege that he shall have justice; and that, at least, every man may expect from God. His ways are equal, though our ways are unequal. Psalm 99:4: "The king's strength [and who is that but God?] also loveth judgment. Thou dost establish equity." So does God, by His rule and His example. Conclude, therefore, whatever His dealing is with you or others, that He is righteous in all His ways and holy in all His works.

The subject cannot always see the reason for his prince's method, nor can a child always see his father's. But when they come to that knowledge, they magnify what before they were ready to misconstrue. Perhaps you do not understand the ways of God towards you or His church; but be silent before Him, for you shall see in the long run that with righteousness He judges the world and the people with equity.

This doctrine pronounces the misery of all hypocrites. For it follows, by the rule of contraries, that with such froward persons God will show Himself froward. He who walks contrary to God shall have God walk contrary to him. The way of hypocrisy, as well as of impenitence, is a way of contrariety to God, whose holy law the hypocrite casts behind his back. It is a way of contrariety to Jesus Christ's prophetic chair, His priestly cross, and His kingly throne—and certainly God will walk contrarily unto them. He will outwit the most subtle and overthrow the most stubborn hypocrite on earth. He overtakes the wise in his own craftiness, and the counsel of the froward is carried headlong. He who will wrestle with God shall feel it first or last.

The vain hypocrite hopes to overreach God, to carry his contrivance cleanly; but let him not be deceived, for God is not mocked. As a man sows, so shall he reap. Job 8:14: "Whose hope shall be cut off, and whose trust shall be a spider's web." You see a spider's web to be a very curious work, but its origin is from a spider's bowels, and its design to catch poor flies. And though she is as secure in it as in a castle, yet, when the broom comes, down they go. The thread that a hypocrite spins is very fine, but it has no higher principle than self, nor any greater end than to deceive. And though he blesses himself in his heart, and sits like a queen in the web that he has spun, yet, when God's broom comes, down he falls into hell, and great is the fall of him.

QUESTION. Who or what is a hypocrite?

ANWER. He is one who has no affection for the nature of religion, and yet has an affectation for the name and reputation of religion. He professes the hatred of sin, and yet cordially loves it. He pretends to love piety, and yet inwardly distastes it. This is a hypocrite, and woe to him. The keenest Scriptures, the sharpest judgments, and the hottest torments are the portion of his

cup. Psalm 18:26 is enough to overwhelm him: "With
the froward Thou wilt show Thyself froward." When infinite patience grows froward, there will be infinite
frowardness. None is so true a Friend, but none is so
fierce an Enemy. God has a peculiar quarrel with proud
men, atheists, and hypocrites; and they shall feel the
weight of His indignation. Alas! Sirs, you drive the
maddest trade on earth: your profession of piety haz-
ards your losing this world, and your practice of
hypocrisy loses you the other—and thus you lose two
worlds for want of one upright heart. Repent, therefore,
quickly of your wickedness and change your course. If
holiness is bad, why do you pretend it? If it is good, why
do you abhor it? What man of reason will put on the
shape of one he hates, when thereby he gets only the
applause of a few and loses the love of many? Alas, you
lose the respect of most on earth by your outside and
the best in heaven by your inside. Oh, therefore,
"cleanse your hands, ye sinners, and purify your hearts,
ye double-minded." Abominate that course that, besides
its own vileness, loses both God and men, and yourselves at the end.

When thieves are being chased, they slip away and
hide themselves in the throng; so when the hypocrite is
threatened but will not be convicted, he therefore al-
leges the following things:

OBJECTION 1. "I am well esteemed, and that among
the best. If I were rotten, surely they would find me out.
I love good people, and they love me; so how can I then
be a hypocrite?"

ANSWER. They judge you by the judgment of charity, but God will judge you with the judgment of verity.
They neither can nor will nor dare be censorious, but
they guess you to be sound within because you are
smooth without. Their great work lies in assuring their
own salvation, and not in questioning others; and so

you may go by them to hell unsuspected, as Judas did by the disciples. They never dreamed of his hypocrisy, but rather suspected themselves; but this did not make his case the safer.

That you love the people of God will be difficult to prove. You like their company, perhaps, for some natural, moral, or acquired excellencies in them; they are well tempered, civil, learned, intelligent, or perhaps of some use to you. But, alas, you hate their holiness, and least like them when they are in their most religious frame. You do not care for their talk of heaven, but you are pleased with their news or discourses upon things on earth. He who loves a holy man for his sanctity loves them all as far as they are holy; and so the holier the person is, the better you will love him.

OBJECTION 2. "I have performed an abundance of duties and have forgone divers sins, and have even continued so to do a great while. Can a hypocrite do so?"

ANSWER. Is there any known duty that lies undischarged by you? And do you delight in the duties you perform as well as do them? Do the precepts of the law please you as well as the promises of the gospel? Do you live in no known sin with purpose, pleasure, and perseverance? It's true, a hypocrite will not always call upon God, but it's hard to say how long he may. Certainly, he will do so while any of his base ends draw him on. Indeed, when sharp troubles come for the cause of religion, then generally such are weary of it and utterly deny that which they never delighted in. Can you now say, in the midst of your multiplied duties, that you would rather do them than not do them? Do you only use prayer, or do you choose prayer? Do you only avoid sin, or do you abhor sin? If these are not true of you, then that Pharisee in Luke 18 shall be justified as soon as you are.

OBJECTION 3. "My own heart does not condemn

me. That is most privy to my own estate, and would be
(surely) most faithful to me in this weighty case. Nay, it
is more against a hypocrite than any other sinner."

ANSWER. Remember that a pacified conscience is
not always a sign of a purified conscience. If conscience is not blinded, it will see; if it is not bribed, it
will speak; if it is not brawny, it will feel. But if it has
been curbed, silenced, and sinned against, it may let
you alone (even as God does) and never bark till it bites
and makes its teeth to meet. There are those who deceive others until at length they be deceived themselves; they have deceived their own hearts so long till a
deceived heart has turned them aside, so that they cannot deliver their souls, nor say, is there not a lie in my
right hand? (Isaiah 44:20)

Do you think in your very conscience that you are an
upright saint and a sincere servant of Jesus Christ? Do
you not know that by yourself which is inconsistent
with integrity of heart? What is that which makes you
tremble at death? Are you more afraid when you hear
thunder than when you hear a searching sermon? And
as for bearing a great hatred to hypocrites, that's nothing; for one proud man may hate another for standing
in his light, and rotten hearts are usually most suspicious and censorious of others. Your best evidence
would be to loathe yourself, and your only cure is to be
pricked at the heart.

Use of Reproof
This reproves those who distrust an upright God.
There is no greater trouble to an upright man than to
be suspected and distrusted, to have his word questioned and his ways misconstrued. Good and upright is
the Lord, and He cannot endure to be called into question. They who know Him will take His word for more
than this world is worth. Psalm 9:10: "They that know

Thy name will put their trust in Thee." But, alas, how few are these!

If we run over those very particulars wherein He shows Himself upright, you shall find much distrust in the world, yea, in the very best. If we are in danger, how few can quiet themselves in God's promise of succour? If we have fallen into temptation, how long ere we can heartily believe our pardon sealed in the blood of Christ? When we begin to pray, which of us believes, that, as sure as we ask, we shall receive? How difficult it is to rely on the grace of God for perseverance, or on the promise of God for all good things in this life and a crown of glory in another? Oh, the wretched distrust of man's heart! Why else do men run to unworthy means to attain their desires every day, and lean no more on Him or His Word than on a weak staff that we dare not trust? You can trust a man when he has money in his hand, and you should trust God when He gives money in the promises. The world should know we serve a God whom we dare trust. The promise is ever as good as the thing promised. He is no flincher with whom you deal. To distrust Him is to divest Him of His dearest attribute, His truth. When we distrust God, we make Him man; when we trust in man, we make him God.

How many experiments have you read, nay, how many experiments have you had of God's uprightness to you? And must they all stand for nothing? What man can come out and say, "I was under such a promise, but I never had the benefit of it? I trusted Jacob's God in vain"? Will you be the first instances of His unfaithfulness? God forbid! For example, what disquieting thoughts have we sometimes had about provision for our children? We think that they will be left succourless and quite forsaken (and unworthy courses are sometimes taken to prevent it); and yet we know they will only become wards of God, and that the generation of the upright shall be blessed.

Here, perhaps, you may reply that you do not so much question God's uprightness as your own. Therefore see in another instance what perplexities God's servants are in for His church when it is rent with schisms, eclipsed with errors, and oppresed with troubles. And yet He has undertaken to rule the world for His church's good, and to see that the gates of hell (stronger than armies on earth) shall never prevail against her. Oh, be silent then; charm down your unbelief and credit these words: "To the upright man, He will show Himself upright."

This also reproves those who dislike upright men. He who is unlike God cannot but dislike both Him and His likeness. Wonder of wickedness, that ever any reasonable creature would hate his Maker's picture; dislike the men who are after God's own heart; and the better the man, the worse it is to hate him. It was so in the beginning, is now, and will be, world without end. 1 Samuel 29:6: "Surely," said Achish to David, "as the Lord liveth, thou hast been upright; nevertheless the Lord favors thee not." Let a man be never so honest, charitable, or unblameable, yet if he reveals his integrity by reproving sin, by a strict watch over his words, by a peaceable demurring at a thing he is unsatisfied with, some of you, though you never saw him or were never disobliged by him, yet out of an inveteracy against God (it can be nothing else), you dislike and declaim against him.

If this man has a hundred excellent qualities, and but one defect or fault, all his good qualities are buried and he goes with you under the notion of his single sin. But on the other hand, let a man be never so ignorant, unclean, a swearer, a drunkard, or an atheist, yet some of you can embrace him and delight in his company—or at least he shall live quietly with you; and, if he does not personally affront you, no magistrate shall ever be informed of him that he might reform him. And (to see your equity) if this man has a hundred ill conditions and but some one good quality, as perhaps of an obliging carriage, all his faults are silenced and he obtains a favorable character from this single virtue. This shows clearly that your spite is directed at the good man because he is good, or else you would cry down other men's faults as well as his.

If pride is bad, or covetousness or passion, why do you not blame them wherever you find them?

OBJECTION. Yes, these things are bad in anyone, but they are intolerable in one who professes more sanctity than others.

ANSWER. His sanctity or profession of it are neither faults nor faulty, but you have an aching tooth at them. And though they aggravate his sins before God, yet I hope with men he may pass better who has but one or two faults than he who has a hundred. And if you are not haters of God, you ought to love him better who has a few errors, and those bewailed (for so all upright men do, though you do not see them) than him who abounds in them and glories in them rather than mourns over them.

OBJECTION. I know your usual saying, that you dislike none but hypocrites, and an upright man you could love in your heart.

ANSWER. Can you prove all them to be hypocrites whom you dislike? And can you justify your suspicion where you can make no proof? I think there is no greater a sign of a hypocrite than easily judging others to be so. But for all your professions, I am persuaded that if Christ Himself were now on earth and should be so severe in His life as never to laugh, so impartial in reproof as to spare neither prince nor priest, so heavenly in His discourse as always to draw it to some spiritual matter, an abundance of Christians would utterly dislike Him, never consort with Him, and would pursue Him to His cross again.

Alas! It is integrity and honesty you hate, and the affront is to God more than to men herein. Is not this hatred without a cause? Is not this to rage at beauty and to have an aversion to innocence itself? Are not these men (such as I have described) the best husbands, the best parents, the best children, the best servants, the best subjects? Proverbs 11:11: "By the blessing of the upright the city is exalted; but it is overthrown by the mouth of the wicked." Oh, relent towards them, and let your love and pity run in the stream with God's. Carry yourselves to them as you think David, Paul, or Christ would do if they were here; and judge in your own consciences whether they would sort with vile swearers in an alehouse or with upright mourners in a chamber. You cannot have a better copy than Him in the text; and therefore, with the upright man, show you yourselves upright.

Use of Examination

Ask your own consciences how needful this is for your comfort here and for your salvation hereafter.

Be exact and serious herein because man's heart by nature is false and froward. It is "deceitful above all things, and desperately wicked" (Jeremiah 17:9). The nature of God, the love of Christ, and the heart of man are inscrutable things. It's true, says Ecclesiastes 7:29, that God made man upright at first. Our faces were directly upon God and our hearts were uniform; but we fell, and now the whole man is turned in quite another way. He who says, "I have always had a good heart," that man never had a good heart! We are estranged from the womb from our God and from our best selves. No cheat is so cunning as the heart of man. It will cry out

as the Pharisee, "I thank God I am not as other hearts
are," when seven abominations are therein. And our
hearts are not only false, but froward. In other diseases
the diseased party is called the patient, and patient they
are to abide the physician's orders. But here the patient
is the greatest disease. What greater misery than a miserable man not commiserating himself? Having to do
therefore with such a piece, what need have you of the
strictest care, so that you may not be bankrupt before
you feel your decay, and broken for want of bruising?

A man may proceed very far and yet prove to be rotten at the heart. He may go nineteen steps and, for
want of going one more step, fall short of heaven. The
young man in Matthew 19 had gone far in keeping six
commandments. Where is the young man who can
come forth and truly say the like? But one thing was
lacking, and that lost all the rest. Consider well how
many changes may pass upon the heart without a thorough saving change: a moral change from debauchery
to civility, a formal change to the profession of godliness, a partial change, a temporary change—but uprightness of heart lies in a hair's breadth. You may hit
the target and yet miss the mark. Consider how far
Herod, Saul, Judas, and others of our acquaintance have
gone and yet have fallen away. We need to sift ourselves
to the bran and put our integrity to the trial.

A man may verily think he is upright, and yet not be
right. Proverbs 30:12: "There is a generation [that is, an
abundance in all ages] that are pure in their own eyes
[they shine illustriously, as the Hebrew word signifies,
in their own opinions and judgments], and yet are not
washed from their filthiness." They were never truly re-
generate. That river of God, the blood of Christ, never
ran through their hearts.

You have heard that he who long deceives others at
last deceives himself, deceiving and being deceived.

This is made plain in the foolish virgins (Matthew 25) who thought their case was good till the gate was shut. A dreadful case, to be damned just at heaven's gates, and to feel hell before we fear it. How blank would a man look who had a sum of money to pay his bills with, and all his money proved to be counterfeit? Even so will many a formal hypocrite look at the last day when all his graces prove to spurious; he has a name to live, but is dead at heart. When the great Judge of heaven and earth shall come with His scales and put those glistering professors into the balance, alas, they will prove to be too light. Weigh that man's faith, then his repentance, then his love; and they are all too light. Alas! Your kingdom has departed from you, and you are a lost man, world without end.

The Marks of an Upright Man

Now if a man verily thinks he is upright and yet prove not to be so, it is high time to come to trial. And though the description which you have had will much supersede this work, and that when all is said, a man who is really upright may most clearly, by reflection and spiritual sensation, find and feel the integrity of his heart, as the mother knows she is with child when she feels it leaping in her womb. Yet, for your further assistance, I shall here give you some clear characteristics of uprightness, and so hasten to an end with this advertisement; if you can lay a sound claim to any one of them, though you should labor to find them all, you may rest with comfort in the safety of your condition, though at present you may not discern the rest. For where there is one integral member of the new man, there is the whole, though not apparent. Do not let one characteristic pass your eye without a faithful trial. Ask yourself, "Is it thus with me?" Do this so that you may know your own selves, know that Jesus Christ is in you, and that you are not reprobates.

1. The first mark of an upright man is that he really approves himself to God. 2 Timothy 2:15: "Study to show thyself approved unto God." This is the care and business of every upright man. In all business and company, his chief care is that the words of his mouth and the thoughts of his heart may be pleasing to God. It is a well-known story of Bernard who, after giving an extraordinary sermon, was found dejected and in the dumps, and after a more sincere, plain discourse the following day was exceedingly cheerful. He told one of his friends who inquired the reason for it all: "Yesterday I preached Bernard, but today I have preached Jesus Christ." Uprightness is when you can say, "Lord, others know my actions, but Thou knowest my ends; others may lift me up too high or cast me down too low, but I am satisfied, if Thou art pleased with me. For not he who commendeth himself is approved, but whom the Lord commends." And this is to walk worthy of the Lord in all pleasing: when a man's great aim is to please God, not to please or exalt himself or others.

But a hypocrite is quite different. Matthew 23:5: "But all their works they do to be seen of men." And therefore they chose trumpets to distribute their alms with, and corners of streets (notice that streets would not serve, but corners of streets) so that two full streets might view them in their prayers. So the poor creatures paid themselves before the great payday: "Verily, I say unto you, they have their reward."

Their thought is, "How will this or that man like this word or action? If such and such commend me and applaud me, I have enough." But the upright man looks at God, and a smile from Him gives him contentment. He may endeavor to compass the good opinion of men, but he will serve God first, and hate any base courses to procure the praise of men. It's part of his character.

Romans 2:29: "Whose praise is not of men, but of God."

2. The second mark of an upright man is that He chiefly loves God. To love the Lord our God with all the heart, with all the soul, with all the strength, and with all the mind is an infallible characteristic of an upright man. When it comes to a disputable case between God and mammon, God and the belly, God and relations, or God and a right eye or hand, if you find (at least for the most part) your soul determining for God, over-ruling the case in His behalf, and that your love for Him can make you condemn the world and all that is in it—fear nothing, you have an upright heart. Try yourself in this: do you use the world to enjoy God, or do you make use of God to enjoy the world? Do you love Him for Himself? Do you love Him like Himself, in everything and above everything?

QUESTION. How can I know that I love Him best?

ANSWER. Has He, if not the most, yet the heartiest of your thoughts? When your ends are raffled to the bottom, do they end with Him or self? Do you love the hours and duties that tend towards Him? Are you troubled that you can love Him no more? Is not heaven itself desirable to you because there you will love Him and hate sin perfectly and eternally? Can you delight in your mercies when you fear they do not come in love? Can you live contentedly under the sense or fear of His absence or displeasure? In a word, does that please you best that tends and ends in His honor, though it shames your persons or crosses your other designs? Do you dearly affect His blessed Word, and those parts thereof that have nothing to commend them to you but their holiness, not only the histories of the Bible, but the doctrines and precepts of the Bible? Can you taste more sweetness in a sermon of Christ, an epistle of Paul, or Psalm 119, than in any human writings in the world? Does the remembrance of your communion

with God and communication from Him more refresh
you than the review of other delights? Song of Solomon
1:4: "We will remember Thy love more than wine; the
upright love Thee." That is a sign of love, and this is a
sign of uprightness.

3. A third sign of an upright man is that He willingly obeys God. 1 Chronicles 28:9: "And thou,
Solomon, my son, serve thou the God of thy fathers
with a perfect heart, and with a willing mind." What he
does, his will is in it. He will do what he can, yea, more
than he can. A hypocrite does more than he would. He
does not act except for profit, credit, and the like; and
when this wind does not blow, he stands as the wind-
mill, stock still. Love to God oils the wheel of obedience, and then a man runs the way of His commandments when the Lord has enlarged his heart (Psalm
119:32). Happy forever is that man whose principle of
motion is within himself.

A hypocrite has no hearty good will to the very duties he performs. He prays, but he has no good will for
prayer; he gives, but his will is another way; his obedience is against his mind. His interest draws him one
way, and his mind goes another. And what a wretched
life must he live, the generality of whose visible actions
go against the frame of his mind, and so neither God
nor himself has pleasure in them (2 Corinthians 8:12).
If there is first a willing mind, the act is accepted by
God according to what a man has and does. Try yourselves therefore: do you find that your wills are pressed
for God? Do you obey your Master as your servants
should obey you, with good will, doing service as to the
Lord and not to men? It is true, you will find another
law, another will drawing the other way; but if you can
say with Paul in Romans 7:22, "I delight in the law of
God after the inward man," then your hearts are upright. If you grieve for your unwillingness; if you bring

your wills to every ordinance, use the means to make them better, and cordially desire to do His will on earth, as it is done in heaven; if the crossness of your will is your greatest burden, and you are gaining ground herein—then your case is good.

4. The fourth mark of an upright man is that he can judiciously appeal to God. "I call God to record on my soul," said Paul—and this not only in a crowd and before others, but in secret in his closet. After consideration of the law of God, and after the survey of his own heart, an upright man (if there is no eclipse upon his spirit) can appeal to the all-searching God in his closet, concerning the uprightness of his heart. This I think few hypocrites can do. Thus Peter could say in John 21:17: "Lord, Thou knowest all things, Thou knowest I love Thee." It is as if he should say, "I appeal from Satan and the world to Thee, whether I do not love Thee above all the world, and above myself; if my heart were opened, Thou would find Jehovah, Jesus, and 'Holiness to the Lord,' written there."

The just man dares appeal to the severest judge, and a sincere saint to an all-seeing God. Psalm 139:23–24: "Search me, O God, and know my heart; try me, and know my thoughts. And see if there be any wicked way in me, and lead me in the way everlasting." So if you can say, "Lord, look at me every way; try me by the light of Thy Word; search me to the quick. I appeal to Thee. Thou knowest I am gold, and not gilded. I am Thine. Thy name is on me and Thy nature is in me. Thou that knowest all things knowest that I love Thee." There is no plainer sign of a cheat than his unwillingness to come to trial; but he who dares bring his heart to the most trying books, to the most searching ministers, to the all-searching God, is sound at heart and a saint within.

5. The fifth mark of an upright man is that he does

not trade in presumptuous sins. Psalm 19:13: "Keep back Thy servant from presumptuous sins; let them not have dominion over me. Then shall I be upright." The tyranny of sin is one thing, the dominion of sin is another. It is the opinion of divines that, though a child of God may have a darling sin, one sin to which he is more inclined than another, yet he does not have a reigning sin, that is, no sin has the absolute command of the whole soul. No, there is a seed of God in a sanctified heart that cannot so yield to sin.

So the difference between the sin of an upright man and another does not lie so much in the nature and kind of the sin committed as it lies in the heart of a sinner. That may be an infirmity in one that is a grosser sin in another. A lesser sin chosen is worse than a greater sin fallen into without choice; a lesser sin allowed is worse than a greater disallowed.

The presumptuous sinner adds the contempt of God to his sin, and so is said to sin with "a high hand" (Numbers 15:30). But the soul that presumptuously reproaches the Lord shall be utterly cut off, and no sacrifice admitted for him. This helps us interpret Hebrews 10:26: "If we sin willfully after we have received the knowledge of the truth, there remaineth no more sacrifice for sins." Both men are opposed to sinning ignorantly, and yet not every sin of knowledge is a presumptuous sin. But when a man knows it to be wrong but does not cares, he heeds neither God nor his will, but lifts up a high hand against Him. It is one thing to sin willingly, another thing to sin willfully. There is something of the will in most sins, but not the whole will. There is a predominant motion of the will toward it, but there is in it a habitual hatred of it. Romans 7:20: "Now if I do what I would not, it is no more I that do it, but sin that dwelleth in me." There is in every sin an interpretative contempt of God; but to create a presumptuous sin, there must be actual presumption and contempt of God. Certainly that man was guilty who was stoned to death for gathering sticks on the Sabbath; and thereupon his tragedy is related immediately upon the law against presumptuous sinners in Numbers 15. An upright man has a radical hatred of sin, and he who hates sin can scarcely sin presumptuously.

6. The last mark of an upright man is that he keeps himself from his own iniquity. You see this in 2 Samuel 22:24: "I also was upright before Him." Oh, then prove it! "I kept myself from mine iniquity." Every man has some sin of his own. We are capable of every sin, but we are not inclined to every sin. Our constitutions usually choose our darling sin; our condition of life or calling may nurse it up. This sin is the trial of our sincerity. A hypocrite chides it before folks, but keeps it under his tongue, cordially favors it, and so makes provision for it. In effect, he prefers it before Christ and heaven. It is this sin that sends most men to hell. They'll part with many things, but a man will give his life for this sin. And there is no wickedness too great to wade through to the fruition of it.

An upright man had, at his conversion, the deepest prick in this vein. The dearer the sin, the dearer it costs in repentance; and thereupon he keeps a jealous eye on it. He is whetted with a holy revenge against it for displeasing such a God as now he finds Him to be, and for hindering so much the comfort of his soul, that he hates this sin and endeavors to prevent and crucify it. He most hates it, though he can least vanquish it. And thereupon he faithfully makes use of all the means he knows to mortify it, and carefully avoids all occasions that may further it. He grieves bitterly for his relapses into it, and gives no rest to his God or his soul till he sees the funeral of it. He is resolved to die in the conflict before he will make peace with it.

Now feel your pulse for the Lord's sake, and do not deceive your own souls. These signs will state your case, if you will but prove your own selves. The explication of them is ours; the application of them is yours. Do not shut the book till you have opened your hearts, and found either the name of a saint or a hypocrite. Why do you retreat? It is not your enemy at the door, but your Physician. To try your case can do no harm. If all is right, you may have the comfort; if all be naught, yet you may have a cure. Do not rush blindfolded into hell. Do not let us put out our best skills in describing characteristics, and then let them alone as you found them for lack of pains. If this does not work, remember we have told you that the clearest sign of a hypocrite is that he dares not come to trial.

Use of Exhortation

Have you made a faithful scrutiny? Then, upon trial, either you find the characteristics of sincerity or not, and you hang in doubt whether you are upright or not. Accordingly, I shall direct my exhortation in three ways:

1. To those who are upright with God

Praise the Lord and be thankful. Psalm 33:1: "Rejoice in the Lord, O ye righteous; for praise is comely for the upright." You of all men have cause to be merry; praise becomes nobody's mouth but yours. Be cheerful in yourselves and thankful to the Lord. What ails you to be lean from day to day who are the King's sons? Who can lay anything to your charge? It is God who justifies. What can dishearten you, seeing the root of the matter is found in you? Turn your complaints into praises. Stand still and admire the distinguishing mercy of God to you, that among so many heathens the Lord should make you Christians; that among so many hypocrites, the Lord should make you upright. Adore electing grace and admire converting grace. Say, "Lord, who am I, naturally a pagan, an errand hypocrite, that Thou shouldst crown me with truth in the inward parts?" And then kneel down and offer Him hundreds of praises; charm up all the daughters of music, your best affections, and tune up your note with angels. Blessing and honor and immortality be given to Him who sits on the Throne, and to the Lamb forevermore. Let heart, lip, and life keep tune; and where your words fail, let your deeds extol His holy name. O Lord, tell me in which way I may honor Thee; and Thou shalt see, Thy grace assisting, that no service shall be too hard for such a wretch to such a God.

Proceed and walk on in your upright way. Hear David in Psalm 26:1: "O Lord, I have walked in mine integrity." Aye, but are you not weary of it, David? Oh, no! Hear him in verse 11: "But as for me, I will walk in mine integrity." It is as if he were saying, "I have done it, and I will do it again. It is enough for sinners to be weary of their ways; but, as for me, I will walk in my integrity." Increase in your uprightness. Job 17:9: "The righteous also shall hold on his way, and he that hath clean hands shall be stronger and stronger." Get ahold of your hypocrisy, and weed it out of your hearts and duties day by day. A little sin is a great burden to him who has a great deal of grace, just as a little spot is to a very cleanly man. Purge out therefore the old leaven, and keep the feast with that dainty fare, the unleavened bread of sincerity and truth. Let nothing bias those honest hearts of yours.

Answer your temptations, that you can do anything but lie, rationalize, and sin against God; that crowns cannot make you betray Christ or wound your consciences; that you fear nobody but God, and nothing in the world but sin. A man of uprightness must be a man of strength.

The more uprightness, the more communion with God; the more uprightness, the more confidence with men; the more uprightness, the more comfort in your own souls. 1 Chronicles 29:17: "I know also, my God, that Thou triest the heart, and hast pleasure in uprightness." Oh, do Him a pleasure, then, by walking in your integrity, and resolve with that upright champion Job in Job 27:5–6: "Till I die, I will not remove my integrity from me. My heart shall not reproach me as long as I live."

2. To those who doubt their uprightness

It is better indeed to doubt with a cause than to be confident without a cause; and better to begin in doubts and end in certainties than to begin in certainties and end in doubts. But take this advice:

Do not sit down quietly in this uncertainty. Who, charged with forgery, will be quiet till he is cleared? In the authority of God's unerring Word, I charge all men with rottenness, corruption, and hypocrisy by nature. If you are true men, clear yourselves, and do not hang between heaven and hell. Who, going a journey, would be content to be ignorant whether he is on the right way or not? You are going on a long journey to eternity; for your own comfort's sake, know whether you are on the way to a holy eternity or a miserable one. It would be best to clear and settle your outward estate. Oh, do not be worse to your souls than you are to your lands; you cannot imagine how far you might go in this work in one month's time, nay, in the spare hours of one month's time. It is a sad case that is threatened in Deuteronomy 28:66: "And thy life shall hang in doubt before thee, and thou shalt fear day and night." Oh, but what is it, then, to have everlasting life hang in doubt before a man; the soul daily takes wings, and you do not know where! Oh, do not sit down quietly with this uncertainty.

Set to clear up your condition by using the proper means. Knock at each minister's door who is near you and borrow light from the wise. When you have a doubtful distemper, you run to the physician; when you have a knot in your deed, you run to the lawyer. But you are demur concerning the state of your souls! Oh, run to the minister! Put on boldness and do not fear; he does not deserve the name of a preacher that is not more glad to have your company than that of the greatest mammonist within his charge. Open your mind freely! "Sir, I am in a great dismay about the state of my soul. This I can say for myself, and this against my self. Deal truly with me, and give out a perfect lot."

Take yourselves to the most searching books; try yourselves by the above named marks. But, above all, take yourselves "to the Law and to the Testimony." But do not be hasty to conclude upon reading any of these, either for or against yourselves without good advice; lest you rush on the rock of presumption or be swallowed up in the quicksand of despair. Get into the right method, and then do not spare any pains. He must give diligence who will make his calling and election sure.

This course has been found useful to some, namely, single out some trying Scripture, for instance, Psalm 119:140. Spend your spare minutes in one day or week to know the true meaning of it. The next day or week compare yourselves by it with all faithfulness: spend another day or week urging all such objections you can justly find against your plea, and a fourth day or week in a sound reply unto them. And then lay them before God, and join your earnest prayer to the Searcher of all hearts to clear and settle you. And, when this is done, try another, and a third. The comfort will be worth the trouble. The answer of a good conscience is worth some serious thoughts, or else it is worth nothing.

3. To those who lack uprightness

Buy this truth and do not sell it. For the love of God, do not be hypocrites. Consider three things:

• Uprightness is amiable in the eyes of God. You see that in 1 Chronicles 29:17: "He hath pleasure in uprightness." You who displease Him by your infirmities need to please Him by your integrity. Song of Solomon 4:7: "Thou art fair, my love," says Christ. "There is no spot in thee." This makes you all fair in His eyes. All the beauty of heaven and earth does not please God as an upright man does; there is no creature like the new creature. And, on the contrary, no sight is as odious to Him as a hypocrite. He who counterfeits the king's coin dies the same death as a rebel. A lukewarm Christian makes Christ's stomach to rise (Revelation 3:16).

• Uprightness is amiable to men. Where enmity to God has not quite razed out all relics of reason and honesty, every man seems to be pleased with integrity; and will speak for such as they think in their consciences mean and speak uprightly. Few would hurt us if we could more sincerely be followers of that which is good. But a hypocrite is odious to all men, like those proto-hypocrites in 1 Thessalonians 2:15 who do not please God and are contrary to all men. He makes an ill choice who embraces a course that God and man both agree to abhor.

Uprightness is comfortable. A sound, upright, good conscience is a continual feast. In troubles, reproaches, sickness, and death, there is no comfort like an upright heart. This will support the spirits, supply the weather-beaten Christian with new spirits, and make him sing in prison when his enemies shall tremble on the throne. This gave the Apostle Paul that boldness before princes to declare that he lived in all good conscience. "Then shall I not be ashamed, when I have respect to all Thy righteous judgments." And, on the contrary, a man has no comfort from hypocrisy, none at all. What joy can a man have when he knows his heart is rotten? What comfort is a velvet patch when it covers a filthy ulcer? What contentment can a man have when he dares not commune with himself? He who is not welcome to his own conscience can be merry nowhere in the world.

• Uprightness is necessary.

It is necessaary to every good duty here. Without it preaching is but a tinkling cymbal, prayer is but as the howling of a dog, and religious discourse is but the prating of a parrot. Nothing is acceptable without it, and goat's hair is a rich present with it. A sincere sigh from him who joins his prayer with integrity is more worth than the feigned eloquence of him who makes the prayer. The two mites of the good widow was more valuable than the great sums cast in by the Pharisees. Our duties are not numbered, but weighed; they are not measured by their length or breadth, but by their profundity. If they are hearty, sincere, and the right stamp upon them, then they are current in heaven. Otherwise, they are but the cutting off of a dog's neck, the offering of swine's flesh, and God abhors them.

It is necessary to our eternal salvation hereafter. Psalm 24:3–4: "Who shall ascend into the hill of the Lord? He that hath clean hands and a pure heart." A man may go to heaven without riches or gifts, but there is no coming there without uprightness. The great question at those gates will be, "Man or woman, where is your oil?" Though men may be deceived, God will not be mocked. He who sows the wind shall reap the whirlwind. In the darkest corner of hell lie the hypocrites. Oh, the rage, horror and torment of a hypocrite in hell! Oh, the confusion and shame that will cover him when his fellow professors shall see him so unexpectedly packed into hell! And what brutish madness is it to make others believe that you are going to heaven, and that while you are stealing into hell!

O sinner, it is absolutely necessary to salvation that you are upright. And therefore, in the name of God, inquire the means to obtain it, and set about them. Well, will you faithfully use them?

The Means to Gain Uprightness

1. Study humility. Habakkuk 2:4: "Behold, his soul that is lifted up is not upright in him." Pride has a great influence into hypocrisy, and humility into uprightness. He who takes pride in being counted great or good, no wonder that he will put on the vizard of more goodness than he has. And, on the other side, he who is content with an ordinary reputation will study to be sound, and not play the white devil to get applause. The humble man concludes, "I am a very weak creature, and I am a very great sinner. What do I care for a golden name when I know that have but a leaden heart?" Study the pure law of God, and then study your impure heart, and be proud if you can. Where can you fine a truer heart than in Paul? Yet he, for his part, is the least of saints and the chief of sinners—although the Lord reckoned him greater than the greatest of the former, and less than the least of the latter. Humility and integrity are born and die together.

2. Be faithful in self-examination. Psalm 77:6: "I communed with mine own heart, and my spirit made diligent search." And to this end, let your consciences be heard; for the spirit of man is the candle of the Lord, to search the innermost parts of the belly. You think that all is right, but when matters come to trial you'll find that all is not. While the sun is under the cloud, you can see no mites in the room; but when its beams shine in, you may see thousands. How do young

people live in the dark, and little feel or fear the plague
that is upon them? But once the light of saving, self-
knowledge breaks in, then Ephraim bemoans himself,
and Paul cries out, "O wretched man that I am!"

For shame, do not live so long as strangers at home.
If a man does not know himself, he knows nothing.
Commune with your own hearts and be still. You commune with God in religious duties; you commune with
men in your civil callings, but when do you commune
with yourselves? Go to the Law; try yourselves by every
command. Luther did this and, beginning with "I am
the Lord thy God," professed that he was so over-
whelmed thereby that he could go no further! Alas,
your confidence flows from your ignorance; one saving
sight of your woeful state would go far in your cure. Oh,
do not lose your souls for want of one serious thought.

3. Get a hatred for hypocrisy and a love for uprightness. Behold them both in their own colors. Read
Matthew 23, and that glass will show you the face of the
one, and Psalm 119 will show you the features of the
other. If you would put the worst badge in the world
upon a man, call him a hypocrite; if you would give any
man the most advantageous title, call him an honest
and upright man. Once you hate hypocrisy, you will flee
it; once you really love uprightness, you'll take pains to
procure it.

Shall I yield to that which my soul hates? Shall I
dwell in a house that I abhor? I'll never do it. May so
rare a jewel as sincerity be had, and shall I live without
it? Shall it be offered to me and I refuse it? No, whatever
it cost me I will not live or die as a hypocrite. Shall I be
a dunghill covered with snow? How odious shall I be
when my show-white mantle will be stripped off? Speak,
man of reason; is simulation lovely? Is dissimulation
amiable? Why will you wear that ugly vizard? Why, for a
name in this world, will you lose a soul in another; for a

shadow of religion lose the substance of salvation? A serious hatred of hypocrisy is not only a means to conquer it, but is a conquest of it. A hearty love for integrity is integrity.

4. Attend a searching ministry. 1 Peter 2:2: "Desire the sincere milk of the Word." He who would attain sincerity must desire God's sincere Word. A searching ministry will make a sound professor; a plain minister will make a plain Christian. Lay your naked heart under the naked truth of God, and let Him write on that blank paper what He pleases. For "the Word of the Lord is quick and powerful, and sharper than any two-edged sword, piercing even to the dividing asunder of soul and spirit, and of the joints and marrow," and is a "discerner of the thoughts and intents of the heart." Such a sword rightly welded will split a hair, and give a man as little rest in formality as in profaneness. The Word of truth is the way to create the grace of truth; the sincere word creates a sincere heart.

The babe draws spirits with the milk, and is nourished thereby. And in the Word truly dispensed, the Spirit is conveyed; and if the Spirit of truth steps in with the Word of truth, then the work is done. Psalm 143:10: "Thy Spirit is good; lead me into the land of uprightness." This good Spirit will take you by the hand, and not only show you, but also bring you into the land of uprightness.

Do not go so much to judge the minister as to be judged by the sermon. Let the most of your severity be employed upon yourselves, and the largest of your charity upon the preacher. The humble, sincere hearer mostly goes home from the preaching with the benefit, while the censorious person goes away with the talk. And remember this: as it requires more grace to hear and profit by a weak or offensive preacher, so a warm and serious spirit will infuse heat and vigor into the most cold, general sermon, if not into the minister.

5. Be instant in prayer. "Every good gift and every perfect gift is from above, and cometh down from the Father of lights." This is a good and perfect gift. Oh, seek it from the Father of lights. The matter of such a prayer pleases Him, and the Mediator pleases Him, and nothing can frustrate it but the man or the matter. Add faith and fervency, and the manner is sure. And then do not let not your suit fall for your own faults, nor lose a prayer for uprightness for want of an honest heart. Beg also the prayers of others. He may hear Job who will not hear his friends. Pray and wrestle till this blessing comes. "O Lord, I have heard such a character of uprightness that I doubt myself. I feel much amiss. I fear all is amiss. I tremble at my condition. I am a Christian by profession, but I am a hypocrite by nature. Thy Word hath found me out and I am lost. Create in me a clean heart, O God, and renew a right, upright spirit within me." And know that the God of Heaven will give grace more freely than an earthly father will bread. Good and upright is the Lord; therefore will He teach sinners in the way.

And thus you have the means. Now, do you mean to use them? What good are directions if you will not be directed by them? Oh, do not let these words stand as your accusers, but your monitors; and remember that practice is the end, the crown of preaching.

Use of Consolation to the Upright

You are blessed men in the mouth of both the law and the gospel. Psalm 119:1: "Blessed are the undefiled in the way, that walk in the Law of the Lord." Matthew 5:8: "Blessed are the pure in heart, for they shall see God." You may be crossed by men, but you shall be blessed by God; you may not see the desire of your hearts in this life, but you shall see God in life everlast-

ing. You may live poor, but you shall die rich. Proverbs
19:1: "Better is the poor that walketh in his integrity
than he that is perverse in his lips, and is a fool." He
who is poor in his wealth but rich in his integrity has a
coin that will pass in the other world. Uprightness and
blessedness are inseparable companions.

OBJECTION. Oh, but sir, that is my fear, that my
heart is rotten at the core and my ways are crooked.
And your discourse has increased my doubts, so that I
fear I do not have one dram of sincerity. And my fears
are increased upon such grounds as these:

• The allegations of Satan. "See," he says, "your rottenness after such a duty, in such a temptation; you
have but a show." And these accusations he follows with
fears and terrors in my spirit, so that my soul is sometimes weary of my life.

RESOLUTION 1. There are roots of hypocrisy in the
sincerest heart; as of all other sins, so of this. Luke 12:1
is remarkable. Jesus began to say to His disciples first of
all, "Take heed and beware of hypocrisy." Christ's own
disciples were in danger of this leaven. All the stock below the grass is perfect crabtree. This you may grant
with grief, and yet retain your integrity with comfort.

RESOLUTION 2. Satan's bills are void in matters of
law, for he accuses the brethren whether they are right
or wrong. He accused upright Job, who had his Maker
as a character witness. The accusation of a condemned
person is no proof in any court of record; yea, his terrors may be your evidences, for he seldom or never
troubles his own house. While his prisoners are quiet
he holds his peace; but when they break away from
him, he shakes his chain after them. But hold up a cru-
cified Christ before his face, and say, "It is this Christ
that I have offended, you fiend of hell. I never sinned
against you. Conquer Him, and then you conquer me!"

• The censures of men. My friends whisper it, my

foes proclaim it, and the minister speaks about me in every sermon. I may be partial to myself, but others will speak plainly.

RESOLUTION 1. The censures of others should make us more severe in trying ourselves. To doubt sincerity is one thing; to try it is another. When they charge the state of hypocrisy upon us, we should mourn for the habits of hypocrisy in us, and then bless God that their opinion for substance is not true. They only say what you might have been. And when your estate is questioned never so unjustly, it is a good way to settle it and make it more sure. And so you will be gainers, not losers, by such surmises.

RESOLUTION 2. While your heart is right with God, do not heed the censures of men. Who was more upright than Job? Yet hypocrisy was his charge, and a hypocrite was his badge; so it was with David, and so our dear Lord Jesus Himself. The malicious world will be sure to charge those faults on you whereof there is no clearing in this life. Resolve with Paul in 1 Corinthians 4:3–4: "But with me it is a very small thing that I should be judged of you, or of man's judgment, but he that judgeth me is the Lord." We shall at last fall to an equal sentence, and till then we have reason to rejoice that we are counted worthy to suffer reproach for His name's sake. Nazianzen said, "We must be dunged with reproaches that we may be more fruitful."

• The cry of my own conscience. And if a man's heart condemns him, who can acquit him? This has always been my fear, and who can clear him who is condemned by himself?

RESOLUTION 1. You must distinguish between dwelling hypocrisy and reigning hypocrisy. Where it only dwells, it is as gravel in the shoe, as the mote in the eye, as the soldier in his quarters. You are weary of it; it makes you halt; you give it no rest; you are very sick of it. But where it reigns, you cannot endure to be touched or searched; it orders your life and actions, and your main design is to cover yourself with God so as to cheat the world.

RESOLUTION 2. Conscience rightly informed may go far in this decision. But conscience is not that which rules the rules, but what which is ruled by the rules. It is like the dial that must be set by the sun of God's Word, and rightly determines only by virtue of that. And sometimes pangs and terrors so overwhelm the conscience that it is not then a competent judge of the cause. If every man whose conscience pricked him was a hypocrite, God help the greatest part of conscientious Christians!

• My sad experience of my dryness in secret duties. I am better in the assembly than in my family, better in my family than in my closet—and it is there that an upright man is best. He who is enlarged and enlivened with others, and straitened in his own bowels, cannot be upright.

RESOLUTION 1. The more company we have in ordinances, the more enlargement we may expect, and yet be upright withal. Our Saviour Himself, when He saw the multitudes, it opened His mouth (Matthew 5:1); and we read but few such sermons from Him as that was. Besides, the numerousness and seriousness of others is a rational means to quicken us who are about the same work. We may expect more of the manifestations of the divine presence where the persons and graces of so many are who are dear to God.

RESOLUTION 2. But every upright man will be serious and hearty in secret, and earnest withal. He would not be hired out of his secret devotions; and a little truth and zeal in a closet is more than the larger expressions of them within a multitude. What is done in secret, provided you do it by choice and in conscience to God, has more genuine features of real integrity than much more in public; for that must proceed from the love of God and His service.

OBJECTION. But I have experience of decay in my soul, and no growth. The path of the just is like the shining light that shines more and more to the perfect day. I feel myself rather worse in every way, not better.

RESOLUTION 1. It is not easy to determine spiritual growth or decay, for its object is various: some grow more visibly in zeal, others in knowledge, others in stability; some more in the roots, some more in the bulk, some more in fruit. And to discern growth is a work of time. Our progress in grace is not so discernable as our entrance into it; for the change here is specific, there only gradual. And the younger children are, the more their growth is discerned.

RESOLUTION 2. A sensible sight of your decay is a true sign of growth; the clearer the sight, the less motes are discerned when there is joined withal a grief for our defects. We grow higher in God's esteem by growing lower in our own. Corruption does not usually reveal corruption, nor does decay reveal decay. If therefore you find that you hate sin heartily and can wisely prevent it, that you can be fully as serious and spiritual in your duties as wise in reproofs, though perhaps not so frequent as heretofore—you have no just cause to charge yourself with decay, much less with dissembling in religion.

OBJECTION. Yea, but I have experience of inconstancy: my soul is in a perpetual state of flux. At one time I burn hot, at another time cold. I am inconstant in avoiding evil and more inconstant in the performance of what is good. This is a hypocrite's temper, and this is mine too.

RESOLUTION 1. A perfect settledness is not to be expected in this life. Our day will have a night; our sunshine will have eclipses. "A sweet hour is a brief hour" has long been an old complaint. Grace that dwells in such a soul, a soul that dwells in such a body, a man that dwells among such variety of business, companies and temptations, cannot escape much variableness and daily alterations. Though you are upright on the way, yet you are but on the way. You are a traveller, not a resident. Heaven is the only state of invariable holiness and happiness.

RESOLUTION 2. The inconstancy of a hypocrite is about the choice of the end, about the very object of the soul; whether he shall choose Christ or corruption, God or mammon. The upright man is fully resolved in this, and his inconstancy is only in the use of means, not whether he should pray or not pray, meditate or not. He does not always have the same degree of love to them, heat and delight in them, or comfort from them. This must be mourned for here, but can be cured only in heaven.

• The deceitfulness of the heart. This is so great that after all my trial I may still be mistaken. There are lamps that may delude a man even to the gates of heaven. And I am sure my heart is one of the worst of the kind, and so most likely to deceive and be deceived.

RESOLUTION 1. Though the heart is deceitful in itself, yet it is discernable by the help of God's Spirit. Jeremiah 17:10: "I, the Lord, search the heart." And He can and will lead every diligent self-searcher into the darkest corners thereof. God and man together may find it out. A carnal, careless eye does not see it, but he who *would* know himself *shall* know himself. No man is deceived here but he who is willing to be deceived.

RESOLUTION 2. As your holy jealousy is a good sign of uprightness, so it is a good antidote against hypocrisy. He who detects a cheat is not then of his party; and he who knows he has a Proteus to deal with will be vigilant over him. He who hates and bewails hypocrisy, and that most in himself, will never die as a hypocrite.

And therefore be of good comfort, you upright ones. Your matter shall stand and your tenure is good, notwithstanding the suits commenced against it. These shaking fits only confirm your health. The greatest tempest does not hurt the tree that is well-rooted; its roots will spread all the more. The pinching, trying frosts strengthen the sound man, and everything does good to him who is good and upright in his heart. However you may be reputed or used in this world, whatever condition concludes you here, yet in life, in death, in judgment, and in eternity, integrity will be a cordial.

Finis